CW00836107

THE

AWKWARD

TRUTH

By

TOMAS JIMENEZ GARCIA

This book is dedicated to

The Mighty ASG[1]

The world is yours, don't let it slip away.

1. Anglo-Scandinavian-Germanic people

Prolouge

All that which is referred to, as 'Western Civilisation' is in reality the sum of the experience of those peoples I have labeled in this book as the ASG. It is generally accepted in this period of political correctness that it is right to suggest that this mighty expression of human progress is enhanced and enriched by the addition of the experiences of the other major racial groups. Nothing could be further from the truth. The acceptance of this philosophy is corrupting and changing the essential nature of the ASG view of life in a manner which if left unchecked will lead inevitably to the destruction of this world changing movement. The consequences of that destruction are illustrated in the following chapters. The mechanical and financial attributes of Western civilisation have been taken on by many countries but outside those countries which are governed by the ASG, none have fully understood the underlying philosophy of this mighty social movement.

The current destruction of Western civilisation can be viewed as it happens now in the society of the USA, which after only seventy years of supreme world power, is in a state of rapid decline. That decline in itself presents enormous dangers to the rest of the world, because as that decline gathers momentum the USA will remain immensely powerful in a military sense and yet will be increasingly administered by poor political judgement.

This book sets out the view that there exist, on this Earth of ours, a number of ***evolutionary*** levels which are contained within the human population. The failure to recognise these different levels for what they are; is currently the mechanism which is destroying the security and well being of all peoples. A supreme example of this blindness is the awful damage visited on the people of England with the frantic embrace of 'multi-culturism' by the liberal minority.

In the historical period before the fifteenth and sixteenth centuries the great races of Earth had lived in relative isolation for up to a million years. It is the view of this writer that in the period of that isolation each of the great racial groups developed in an evolutionary sense quite differently from each other. This writer believes that their performance as races today clearly reflect those different evolutionary values.

Thus it was that in the pre-fifteenth century, the Chinese in their geographical isolation, the Negro in his sub Saharan enclave, the South American Indian in his isolated continent, the Euro-Asian sandwiched between Europe and China and the Arab around the Mediterranean. All of these peoples lived for up to a million years in this isolation and developed quite different ways of life. These developments, some attractive and some unattractive, have nothing to do with intelligence; they are the result of the common human intellectual capacity reacting to uncommon and quite different environments.

Approximately twenty-five thousand years ago there arose in North Central Europe, again in response to a particularly harsh environment, an energetic and extraordinarily capable people. Growing in strength and numbers these people pushed westward steadily. They overwhelmed and eliminated the Celtic type peoples already inhabiting these regions and submerged the whole of North Western Europe and Scandinavia with their new energy. Some fifteen hundred years ago successive waves of invaders from this racial group occupied the country we now call England. The people created by this great historical movement, I have labeled the ASG (Anglo Scandinavian Germanic Peoples). This group of people created what we now like to call Western Civilisation.

The 'Little Blue Book' attempts to warn the people of the Western world of the immense danger that their civilisation stands in and yet suggests that all is not yet lost.

I have no doubt that unscrupulous people will use the words of this book to justify acts of violent discrimination against ethnic minority groups. Such action is against the fundamental social philosophy of the ASG. All racial groups, from whichever level of evolution, have a part to play in the future of mankind. However it is vitally necessary for us to recognise the fundamental differences between these groups and ensure that particular evolved abilities are used in the interest of all peoples.

When examining the performance of the different racial groups throughout history the inexorable conclusion at the end of that examination is that these racial groups behave in quite different ways to common stimuli.

Unfortunately, because 'Race' in the twentieth century has been the subject of an incredibly successful 'Taboo,' serious discussion on all matters of race have simply not taken place. The consequences of that Taboo which grew out of the revulsion felt worldwide at what happened in the 'Holocaust' are potentially incredibly disastrous. This book seeks to explain where these differences arise.

It is important to remember that any study of racial differences has nothing whatsoever to do with skin pigmentation. The colour of a man's skin is a consequence of an evolutionary source located in a hot climate. Skin colour has no significance other than evolutionary protection against the sun's rays. Fundamental racial differences such as, intellectual awareness, social responsibility and social creativity are the consequence of differing evolutionary paths creating unique gene assemblies. Any denial of this essential truth is simply unintelligent.

CONTENTS

PART ONE

CONTENTS

PART TWO

THE REALITY OF GENES

No one can escape the consequences or the benefit of their genes. The genes, which decide who and what you are at birth, will decide whether you are tall or short, dark skinned or fair skinned, intelligent or stupid, whether you will have a healthy body or be racked by the evils of congenital disease. All that you achieve in life will be as a first consequence directly due to your genetic makeup at birth. To ignore the reality of the genetic makeup of a person or of a people is a recipe for disaster. All of us, who live in the West today, stand on the brink of such a disaster.

TOMAS

6TH JANUARY 2000

FOREWORD

This small book seeks to explain the wide range of human behavioural characteristics that are evident in the various races that populate the earth. All mankind, within its variety of racial groups, has shared a universal benefit in terms of time experienced on the planet, why then are there such enormous differences in group behaviour?

In this small book I briefly examine the Diaspora in the geographical journey of man, we ask the question, where did man came from and how did he make that journey. In particular I look carefully at the fundamentals of environment and suggest that there is a separate strand of evolution that influences the way that particular group minds work. There are clear successes and failures within the racial groups and I have had a closer look at some of these and in particular have illustrated the failure of the Negro people to produce effective societies.

I later invite you to look at the imminent prospect of the complete failure of Western civilisation and it is clear that there exists an identifiable condition of 'over civilisation'. This affects people who live in communities that have achieved high levels of performance and developed compassion and welfare care to very significant levels in their particular society. These people assume, and of course, often wrongly assume, that because they and their neighbours share this caring compassionate attitude to life, then all humans must share it also. The evidence, I suggest, says that this is not true and I believe this erroneous belief is one of the primary contributors to international decay.

One of the ever-present phenomena that distort human behaviour is religion. In this twenty-first century the Moslem faith has a profile which we cannot ignore. In this book I ask the question, can the Christianity of the West and the values of Christianity if not the ritual, coexist with the growing power of the Moslem faith in social harmony? I conclude that it cannot.

Because the discussion of race has been subject to an extraordinary taboo, the effects of the resultant non-discussion have created enormous dangers for the civilisation of the West. It may not be too late to overcome these dangers; certainly if corrective action is not taken quickly the gloomier forecasts of this book will certainly apply.

Tragically, the great crisis in the breakdown of the ASG socially and racially comes within the century when easily obtained and inexpensive oil finally runs out. I look at the effect of the end of oil and make some predictions on the future of this century.

THE HUMAN JOURNEY

CHAPTER ONE.

ALL MEN ARE CREATED EQUAL

This attractive, but totally erroneous statement, forms part of the great American legend. It is a base line, which has been used to determine the way in which the nations of the world have attempted to deal with one another for most of the past two hundred years.

The tragic reality is that all men are not created equal, either physically or in their ability to use the standard human brain that is present in all human beings. This book examines the differences between identifiable races and seeks to explain those differences by applying the simple rules of evolution. The conclusions drawn from this study strike at the heart of all Western political thinking and if accepted will change the future nature of human society.

It is my position that the very existence of the philosophy of equality of peoples in all things is the greatest threat to a beneficial future for the all members of the human race.

When considering the conditioning of the human species which can justly be called evolutionary consciousness, it is necessary to continually have in mind the fact that the palaeontologists and anthropologists all aver that the basic human brain capacity is common to all of the varieties of human beings on the planet.

With this fact in mind, this book is not about investigating evolutionary intelligence, it is about investigating the evolutionary changes that occur in the “mind” of man. I seek to make no judgement on comparative intelligence of different races. I begin with the clear presumption that ‘mind’ and ‘intelligence’ are not necessarily a measure of each other. I am in fact investigating, the differences that the use of the "standard computer" which is the human brain, demonstrate in particular human groups. Given that I liken the human brain to a standard piece of equipment i.e. the computer, then the example of the computer can be used when looking at the differing levels of use we put that piece of equipment to.

The average family computer is rarely used for more than mediocre tasks and is rarely programmed to achieve anything more significant. Of course we can raise the range of output of the computer by plugging in and adding more advanced software programmes. The basic capability (Brain)) of the home computer is sufficiently wide to easily accommodate such extensions and does not require additional 'brain' power; we just plug in more 'mind'. Unfortunately the mechanism we have for updating the standard human brain with advanced mind programmes can only be done by genetic addition. There is clear evidence that the acquisition of information by learning is simply not efficient in realising human value mind changes. There is no means of plugging in and swapping that information in respect of human beings. Remember always that this is not about learning the mechanics of any science or learning the means by which human beings perform any particular tasks. What is being considered is the way in which all of that information which can be "learned" is employed in life against the background and the disposition of the human mind.

It is probable that any average member, of any of the races present in the human population can, given adequate training, perform efficiently almost any [1]mechanical task that is performed by man as a species. What is clear however is that the use to which that capability is put is subject to a very different aspect of human behaviour. It is the purpose of this book to demonstrate that this factor has nothing whatsoever to do with the mechanical ability to learn tasks or store information. That condition which is mistakenly called intelligence. It is a fatal mistake to believe that the evolutionary experience of the mind can be passed on simply

[1] Mechanical in this context mans any hand and eye task and includes artistic expression.

by instruction. All the available evidence suggests that this is not so.

In the 20th/21st centuries we have been conditioned by the mindless liberal avalanche to believe that all human beings, irrespective of racial origin are equal in all things. We have also been led to believe that if a particular race is not performing to standard, then if we throw enough money or educational programmes at the deprived human group we are certain to achieve the kind of progress which we ourselves in the great Western societies expect as a right. Reality is much more complicated. For instance, Western society, or more accurately Western media, has convinced itself that the reason that let us say the Arabs of Iran behave in the way that they do, is because they have somehow been deprived of the mechanisms of education, freedom, political democracy and social solvency. Is this belief reasonable when we consider that Iran has been in touch with the major Western civilisations for upward of 2000 years? Indeed the territory we now call Iran, was itself part of one of the earliest societies organised by man. That social experience taking place long before Europe arose from the primeval heap. Especially why is it reasonable in this early part of the 21st century when oil revenue should have made the Iranians among the wealthiest and happiest people on Earth? No, such an answer is not reasonable; the real answer is much more fundamental. The Iranians as members of their particular racial group behave as they do because the mind conditioning which they have inherited as a consequence of their distinctly separate evolutionary path ensures that they act in this way and gives them no choice to act in any other.

In this book we look at some of the great racial groups and consider their performance on the stage of humanity. I have examined some of the groups more closely than others because of the inaccurate perception of human behaviour, which is commonplace in our society. I have illustrated the failure of the Negro with more detail than other races because most of our liberal/humanistic thinkers, almost without exception, have illustrated the Negro as the most sinned against and exploited people in the great panorama of mankind. The truth emerges to any dispassionate observer as a clear demonstration that the Negro is incapable of good government or human value societies and will whenever tested; revert to their evolutionary status of hunter-gatherer.

The Negro condition is not a mystery but the simple result of his inherited evolutionary status. He cannot be blamed for this state of mind, it is the only one he has.

<u>CHAPTER TWO.</u>

<u>THE DIASPORA OF MANKIND</u>

Man has always sought an explanation of his origins, "Where did all life come from?" This question and its flawed answers have generated most of the world's religions and the mystery of creation has continued to occupy the minds of theologists and philosophers throughout the history of mankind. Unfortunately, because man's intellect is unable to accept the concept of there ever having been a state of 'nothing' a 'nowhere' or a 'no-when', man had to invent a supernatural being or condition to attribute creation too. In the mind of man, everything and every condition must have a beginning and an end and the provision of endless gods not subject to natural laws was the only solution.

Mans invention of the concept of 'God' is by itself a handicap to the progression of mankind. Having a 'God' gives humanity an excuse to lay off responsibility for uncomfortable events. A belief in divine purpose means real problems requiring real physical solutions can be left to chance. The almighty will provide. All, without exception, who wear the robes of religion, are charlatans, perpetuating a falsehood and denying the truth. It is no surprise that throughout history the established churches have resisted great movements of change whether it be the denial of the earth's passage around the sun or the incontrovertible truth of evolution.

During the nineteenth century the huge debate generated by Charles Darwin's theory of evolution split intellectual opinion in the Europe of that time. It also attracted the most vitriolic hostility from the Churches. It is difficult now to begin to appreciate how otherwise intelligent men could possibly deny the revelation of evolution once it had been described and yet we are today faced with a similar denial of self-evident truth in the matter of the Human race. ***It is the writer's belief that the***

Human race exists in a variety of evolutionary levels on the surface of the world that we know, as does every other form of animal life.

Darwinian evolutionary results can only be generated over very long periods and in the two million or so years of the human Diaspora; we have a_period, which is just long enough to have generated significant change in the basic human animal which began the Diaspora.

The most significant factor in evolutionary change is environment, and the distinct racial groups identified in this treatise, have each responded to quite clearly defined and markedly different climatic and geographic conditions. Each of the groups has spent most of the evolutionary period since the Diaspora in relative isolation from the other groups. This isolation brought about by natural geographical physical barriers.

So where did it all begin? Within the scientific community it is now rarely questioned that the teeming diversity of the human race is descended from a single parent race, and again it is now generally accepted that it is likely that that parent race was the direct ancestor of the Negro at that time located in Central/East Africa. Certainly the best archaeological evidence that we have suggests that this is probably so. Whether by an accident of mutation or by environmental pressures, the first humans on this planet who took that mighty step above the great ape society, probably did so somewhere in East Central Africa. The Diaspora of the human race from central Africa to its world dominating position in modern times took a long time; evidence suggests that we may be looking at a period of around three million years. Others will suggest up to five and a half million years.

If we assume that the archaeologists are correct and mankind did first appear in what is now known as Eastern Central Africa below the Sahara, it seems likely that the first wave of the Diaspora was simply northwards to the shores of the Mediterranean. It is probable that each wave of the Diaspora was brought about by group conflicts among the existing settled group leading to the expulsion of defeated tribes or families who were consequently driven to seek new places to live. Alternatively, of course, simple growth in population pressure will have led to a continuous trickle of families seeking hunting preserves of their own.

The parent group, the Negro, stayed behind the barrier of the Sahara in splendid isolation until the sixteenth/seventeenth century when Western Europeans began to seriously explore the world. The Negro lived in an environment where apart from cyclic natural disasters, food was plentiful and the climate hospitable. These two factors created an environment, which contained little pressure to change. The environment required strong, physically able people to hunt the plentiful game. Shelter was not a requirement for survival, only for comfort and defence and as a consequence, shelter developed in only the most rudimentary fashion. With game and fruit plentiful, there existed in this environment no pressure to create sophisticated agriculture, so non-emerged. Darwin's theory of evolution depends totally on there being the pressure of necessity to accept change in order to operate. Despite being surrounded on three sides by Ocean, the Negro developed no shipping profile. Even the wheel covered Africa only after colonisation by the Europeans. Without environmental pressure to change, nature is content with the status quo.

It seems likely that the first wave of the Diaspora over the next hundreds/thousands of years spread out along the southern shores of the Mediterranean and then Eastward into what became known in our time as the Middle East. This movement route is likely because of the pedestrian nature of this immigration across convenient land bridges. This first wave of the Diaspora would over the long centuries evolve into the people we now call Arab. The Arab ancestor found himself in quite a different climatic environment to that left behind in Central Africa and an environment where game herds were only a minor source of food. Fish stocks were plentiful, and so quickly we would have seen the development of boats and ships. The relatively tranquil Mediterranean was an ideal sea for Mans early experiments in sail.

The need for food and the accident of discovery meant the development of agriculture. Concentration on agriculture requires barter and the creation of commerce. Commerce inevitably creates surplus wealth and surplus wealth creates leisure and society. Leaders of any form of society, seek easily identifiable symbols of their power, so the pressure to illustrate that power with architecture and art is generated. Obviously this new and sophisticated environment would require that its exploiters would be intellectually able rather than physically strong and in the Darwinian game of natural selection, the intellectually able would, among the Arabs, come to the front and dominate. The less intellectually able would fall to the bottom of the social ladder as slaves or as labour. These evolutionary pressures on this first wave of the Diaspora influenced the development of an organised, intellectually curious people, well able to deal with the natural problems of survival and progress. And whilst the Arab of today is probably the direct descendent of this first wave of the Diaspora; then it is interesting and informative that the Arab has climbed further up the tree of mental/mind evolution than the descendants of some of those peoples involved in much later waves of the Diaspora. This higher development is probably due to almost continuous exposure to other evolutionary level peoples.

It is probable that the spread of peoples throughout the entire area of Southern Europe, Asia and the Malaysian archipelago was achieved whilst the human animal existed on a mere subsistence level and was largely complete at about 100.000 years ago. Migration would have been arbitrary and spasmodic, driven and depending on the pressures of conflict, famine or drought. However, after many thousands of years, the human animal was_established on all easily reached landmasses. Dominant local populations, without consciousness, used natural barriers to seal their areas of influence, and the great settled period of the world-wide human population began. In this period the Chinese were alone in their Eastern locality, the Indian locked into their own subcontinent below the Himalayas, the Negro behind the barrier of the Sahara Desert, and so on. The superficial different physical appearances of the primary racial groups will have developed in this long settled period. These different appearances will have had their roots in the particular gene bank of its earliest colonists, emphasising the characteristics of the original group by the necessary early inbreeding and also influenced by climate and diet. The sun resistant black skin of the Negro will have had little benefit to the northern settlers and a trait that bestows no advantage is soon overtaken by more productive strains. This sun resisting black skin advantage is not normally found in humans living naturally north of the tropics.

Sometime, relatively late during this Diaspora, perhaps 15,000 to 30,000 years ago, humans (Genus Homo Sapiens) began to move into the area that we now know as North Western Europe. There had existed in this area a pre-Homo Sapiens's human population that we call Neanderthal. Although we know little of this time there would certainly have been bloody conflict between Homo Sapiens settlers and the Neandertaller. The Homo-Sapiens colonisation movement would almost certainly have occurred involuntarily, for who would willingly forsake the sunlit welcome of the Northern Mediterranean area for the cold and inhospitable northern climes. Remember that with the period under discussion closer by 10 millennium to the retreating Ice Age than are modern times, the North West of Europe would have been much more inhospitable than in this present century. The movement into the Northwest was probably either the result of tribal conflict leading to expulsion with the defeated tribes or families moving northward or westward away from danger, or perhaps the reasons were once again only the simple pressures of_population. Whichever of these forces were at work, the movement began.

For the early settlers in this North Western region, life would have been incredibly hard, and the harshness of this environment began to work through inevitable natural selection on those early settlers. Death would have been an ever-present shadow on a society living in an unforgiving landscape and only the very fittest and most able would survive. Shelter was imperative. Those who couldn't build a shelter would die in the harsh winters, husbandry was critical, no food grew when the winter winds blew and only the clever and organised who stored food for the winter would eat and survive. In this harsh unforgiving environment the Darwinian process created the ASG, Tall, physically strong, energetic and resourceful; the qualities that would lead this latecomer to the human fold to dominate the Earth were being put in place. The need to rely on family and tribal resource against a pitiless environment in this developing community also saw the creation of softer human trends, which in the fullness of time would emerge within their society as structured compassion and community care.

Unlike the earlier societies in Egypt, the Middle East, India and China, the ASG existed for most of their history in tribal or family units. Coming late to the table of civilisation they learned quickly and were able to assimilate and improve ideas in respect of social organisation, architecture and military organisation. The ASG stepped into civilisation without the mind-crippling burden of societies organised on slavery and repression. The tribal bodies from which the ASG sprang were free thinking participative structures in a form absolutely essential to the environment from which they were given birth.

At about the time that the first settlers were arriving in the northern forests, three of the earlier waves of the Diaspora, with centuries of settlement behind them were making the first moves toward organised society. In the Middle East, in Northern India and in Eastern China, communities were struggling toward structured civilisations. This process with many setbacks continued for centuries and in these named areas the first cities and first managed economies would shortly appear.

Whilst some societies were advancing toward social enlightenment, some of the Diaspora waves were less successful. At sometime in the prehistory period, early settlers had landed on the Australian continent and for the remainder of human history until overtaken by the European invasion, would remain in their prehistory state. The Aboriginal failure to develop probably happened for exactly the same reason as the Negro failure. This group lived in a land with plentiful game, abundant fruit, and a climate that required no shelter. As a consequence there was no pressure to change. It is interesting that the aboriginal never experienced a population explosion; this in itself avoided at least one level of environmental pressure. When Europeans first arrived in this huge country it was very sparsely populated. One simple reason why this was so, may have been simply the inevitable result of low levels of fertility. We know of course that dynamic population growths are nearly always associated with the development of agriculture and the aboriginal did not develop agriculture. Whatever the reason, the_result was of course that the pressures of population felt in most other areas of the human colonisation of the Earth never happened in Australia. Without development pressures of any kind, the Aboriginal in a bountiful land, developed neither recognisable society nor agriculture, written language or commerce. He remained an uncomplicated hunter-gatherer in the traditions of the earliest peoples. The modern day Australian anthropologists, clinging to political correctness, like to point out that the aborigine can find food under rocks where white men can't. Such a talent in no ways justifies the sole occupation of one of the Worlds great continents for over 20.000 years.

When the ASG were beginning their colonisation of the Northwest, yet another group of humans went even further north. These settlers pushed up into the land of permanent snows and in this bleak and forbidding landscape the people including those known as the Inuit would develop. (I include all members of the 'Thule and Dorset cultures together with the Tuniit peoples in the term Inuit). (Anyone who doesn't believe in human evolution should compare the body fat of an Inuit compared with a Mediterranean dweller.) This austere landscape practically froze out development due to survival pressure, which meant continuous involvement with the acquisition of food and warmth, and the absence of any material other than snow.

It would seem that some members of the Inuit/Mongol peoples might have made it back to warmth and a better life by using the ice route into North America. Between 15 and 25 thousand years ago these Inuit/Mongol migrants were probably the ancestors of the Red Indian. Red Indian and Mongol peoples share many DNA characteristics. The Red Indian is another example of the failure of some Diaspora waves to develop toward society and civilisation. Although Hollywood has with its typical ingenuity, created a culture and invented traditions for the Red Indian, the truth is that the Red Indian remained a Neolithic savage, with no attractive aspects to the brutal homicidal fratricide practised as standard by the scattered tribes. The Red Indian lived in one of nature's most benevolent lands, yet added nothing to it and failed to exploit its wealth. Neither writing nor the wheel was developed and shelter was embryonic and non-permanent. In no other area of human colonisation has a period of 25 thousand years in a bountiful environment been so unproductive. In the case of the re-engineered profile of the Red Indian it is interesting to note how modern politically correct media seeks to alter human images to satisfy flawed philosophies. If you visit the site of the Pilgrim Fathers landing place in Plymouth Massachusetts, you may be struck, as I was when I first visited this area, by the concentration of information on the perceived bad effect that the settlers had on the local Indian population rather than on the giant groundbreaking role of these early pioneers. Above the landing site in Plymouth is a statue of an Indian chief. Curiously, he is tall and slim with a noble European face and chiselled nose. Extraordinary when you consider that the real chief,_had he been_portrayed accurately, would have had a spatulate nose, be about 5 foot seven inches tall, and would have been wearing little of the 'Hollywood' clothing that adorns the statue. This is a dishonest and quite regular condition that is experienced when modern society looks at and cannot accept a 'failed' human group. This philosophy is generated by the politically correct belief that it is not possible to have a failed human group. The interested parties generate dishonest human sympathy by illustrating the failed racial group as simply a European in exotic clothes.

The Red Indian was not a noble savage; he was not an environmentally aware savage. (He would routinely fire the prairie or drive herds of buffalo over a cliff although only needing one carcass for food) He was an evolutionary retard living in a hideous non-developing society based on murderous tribal warfare.

The peoples who inhabited South America prior to Columbus appear most likely to have made the journey across the Pacific from Asia. It has to be said however that they have no genetic relationship with the Polynesian. Some historians prefer to suggest that these peoples came the overland route from the Bering straits, but there is no genetic evidence that this is so. And if these people had indeed travelled this route, there is no archaeological evidence for such a trail. To me it is inconceivable that the South American colonising group could have passed through the bountiful lands of what we now call the USA and not put down roots. Such a journey would have meant travelling through a benevolent climate and fertile land. Then, leaving this semi paradise behind they would make the crossing of the Mexican deserts and continuing through the narrow isthmus between North and South America. Such a journey would be extremely unlikely. How the real journey from Asia was accomplished, by accident or design we may never know. It certainly occurred before the emergence of writing or the wheel in Asia because there was no transfer of either of those skills with the first settlers into this bountiful land.

Having arrived in the fertile and benevolent lands of the South American continent, the migrants went on to develop significant civilisations. Tragically, the civilisations of South America are certainly among the least attractive of all major human developments. Embodied in these civilisations, a level of brutality and human depravity marks one of humanities failures. The organised and systematic murder of people in this period and in this place is unprecedented in history. In one authenticated account the Aztec chronicle and record, as a simple matter of fact, the murder of 40 thousand innocent people over a period of four days, this is just one of thousands of such mass murders. The queues waiting to die must have stretched for miles.

The last great wave of human colonisation was the Polynesian exodus across the Pacific Islands, this final wave of settlement happened too recently to be allowed the breathing space that evolution requires. European explorers overtook the Polynesians before they reached their majority.

This is a very brief thumbnail sketch of the gigantic two to three million-year panorama of the Human Diaspora but this sketch illustrates in quite simple terms the mechanics of human colonisation of the world.

Philosophers and devotees of religious cults seek to explain mans purpose with convoluted theories, the truth is much simpler, Man is simply the Earth got up articulate and all the history of life on Earth the result of that inchoate evolutionary search for identity and purpose.

CHAPTER THREE

ISOLATION AND EVOLUTION

Following the Diaspora, the separate races of mankind settled into their isolated areas of development and were largely undisturbed over a hundred thousand years. It is inconceivable to any reasonable thinker, given the rules that govern evolution, that this long isolation should not have encouraged and actually generated evolutionary change.

It is my belief that to any dispassionate observer the human race lies clearly exposed in several levels of evolution. To deny this truth is simply dishonest and to ignore it can destroy nations. This destruction is clearly illustrated in history. For instance; many people have sought an explanation for the disappearance of the mighty Roman Empire. How can a people and a society, so talented, so organised, so powerful, then degenerate into the little regarded backwater of human power, which Italy has become? The simple answer is of course, that the Romans did ***actually, physically, disappear*** in the genetic sense, bred out of existence by the presence of millions of slaves whose genetic background came from at least four other evolutionary levels. In the time of the early Imperial period, for every freeborn Roman_in Italy, there lived a thousand slaves. The people of Italy today, and indeed most of those whom we call Latin, are the product of those slave populations and the genius of the Roman provides only perhaps .001% of the gene strain in those countries. With that inevitable assimilation of the slave population, Roman genius was extinguished.

Roman genius was extinguished by the importation of slaves from a number of evolutionary levels. The past importation of slaves from Africa and the importation of all of the differing levels of evolution in the modern epoch is currently destroying the USA, which was built by the ASG. The USA will not have Rome's 1000-year history.

Any intellectual discussion of race has nothing whatsoever to do with colour. For the Liberal Bigots let me say that again. ***Any intellectual discussion of race has nothing whatsoever to do with colour***. Race is about the genetic makeup of different evolutionary human groups and skin pigmentation is immaterial.

I believe that in any circumstance where a mass of people are isolated from the other peoples of the earth for any extended period then that group will inevitably develop behavioural differences. It follows that if my identification of evolutionary differences in Human groups is valid; we are led to a position, which suggests a Hierarchy of mankind in evolutionary values. In a simplistic sense this would create a table where if physical strength is to be the required measure, then the Negro people will stand in the highest evolved position.

However, whilst making assumptions based on evolution, it is absolutely necessary when talking about the word itself, to have a common view on what precisely the term evolution really means.

WHAT DO WE MEAN BY THE TERM EVOLUTION?

Evolution is a mechanism which nature has used to ensure the survival, by adaptive change, of a myriad of species throughout the long years since life first appeared on Earth. It is a word used by men to account for the enormous variety of animal and plant life that exists on Earth. Used to account for, in the sense that it describes a process, which leads to continuous change in all life forms that are exposed to environments that are themselves changing. Charles Darwin (1809-82) first published in 1859 his gigantic mold shattering book "On the Origin of Species by Natural Selection". This publication identifies in mature form, a theory that is accepted by all intelligent thinkers in the modern age. The publication raised a storm of controversy but is still, in its original form, completely satisfying to any discriminating reader. This publication should be a compulsory read for all schoolchildren.

Darwin's theory of evolution provided science with a satisfactory solution to the origin and also to the differences that exist in the enormous variety of living things that exist on this planet. He explained that over aeons of time, reaction to environmental stimuli produced changes in any living structure in the struggle to survive. The term, survival of the fittest, although prostituted to mean less honourable things today, adequately sums up the struggle of evolution.

We can take the example of the Lion and the Wildebeest as an easily illustrated evolutionary mechanism. Each day that passes in Africa, the Lion hunts the herds of Wildebeest that constantly roam the territory of the Lion. The resulting constant attrition means that in general the slowest or most stupid of the Wildebeest are caught and eaten by the lion, similarly the fastest and most intelligent Lion will be the most successful and most certain in catching the Wildebeest. In both the predator camp and in the hunted camp, this single daily reality means that only the fastest and most intelligent of both species survive to reproduce. Among the Lions and among the Wildebeest, this means there is a constant reselection of the gene hive toward those who are the most able. The inevitable consequence of this progressive reality is that both of these animals will slowly become faster and stronger. If you were in a position to measure the speed performance of the Lion and the Wildebeest over thousands of years, you could certainly measure an appreciable increase in speed and strength. Similarly, if you could return backwards in history by a couple of thousand years, your measurements would show slower and less powerful members of both groups of animals (Always providing that the environment has remained the same)

When to use the word evolution also needs careful consideration, and for instance, children are often misled in considering evolution by the use of the word 'change'. Very often when applied to the differences in a species over aeons of time the word 'change' can suggest sudden and almost magical transformation. The reality is much more prosaic, with minute, sometimes minuscule, differences in individual members of a species giving that individual member a survival advantage, which by improved survival statistics, is then transmitted more widely to the next generation. This endless minute modification continues as long as the species and environment exist. The process can and will be accelerated when environmental circumstances provide unavoidable survival threats.

Of course, until the moment when the first humans stepped into the echoing vestibule of eternity, evolution was a fairly straightforward mechanism. Those birds developed to catch fish and these birds developed to eat insects, this great cat developed stripes to survive in the jungle and that great cat developed a sandy coat to survive on the plains. The Eco-diversity of endless species gratefully fulfilled the needs of survival and any developed conflict would generally mean extinction of the loser. ***With the advent of mankind came the ability for the different levels of evolution of the human species to recognise the advantages of the higher level and to aspire to those advantages.*** This was something completely new to evolution. The fisher bird did not envy the anteater his ants or the tiger the domain and sandy plain of the lion. The human animal with his memory and developed sense of desire is able to generate a wish to be as his more able distant cousins are. All levels of human evolution are able to interbreed and this reality has constantly destroyed and retarded the development of mankind over the whole period of recorded history. We are accelerating this process in this current time and as a result now stand on the edge of a second Dark Age.

The modification of performance, intelligence, strength and size in the mechanism of evolution can be extremely slow or much quicker depending on the rate of environmental change faced by the species affected. Thus we have 55 millions of years from Eohippus (the first horse) to Shergar, but three to seven million years only, from great ape to mankind. The rapidity of the human development is probably due to the fact that human populations in the original Diaspora continually placed themselves in different environmental conditions. We have also to remember that from time to time evolution can be accelerated by mutations. A mutation is a change that naturally occurs in a species as a result of gene malformation. If the change is a beneficial one, evolution will be accelerated by the successful use of the benefit bestowed. Most mutations are however not beneficial and disappear with the single holder of the deformation.

Unfortunately, the present reality of mankind is that the process of evolution toward improvement is being stultified, in that successful levels of evolution are constantly regressed by the assimilation of less successful levels. Out of the less able gene hive then created and over many hundreds of years, a new evolutionary group emerges. This new group will then attract the less successful levels then extant and the process goes round and round. The special problem this time round is that the regressive changes are occurring at a time of critical human crisis. The world population that we have built today is totally dependent on a level of food production, which is only possible because of the availability of fossil fuels and applied technology. This, the twenty-first century, is the century in which fossil fuels will begin to be exhausted. Without a structured approach by all nations of the world to this coming apocalypse, the death of millions will be certain. With the current destruction of the ASG now well advanced, it is likely that no such preparation will take place.

However to move from an understanding of how evolution works, what does that mean in the history of the human race? If we accept the reality of Darwin's theories, it is surely not possible to argue that the great physical separation of the primary human races and their isolated encapsulation in very different environments will have had no effect on individual racial development. The physical separation of these races after all, lasted between one hundred thousand to two million years. It is worth noticing that many of the changes noticed by Darwin on the Galapagos Islands had occurred in less than 100.000 years.

Palaeontology or the physical study of our human ancestry could only begin in a meaningful way after the publication of Darwin's theory. Prior to Darwin's publication it was generally accepted that the human race came fully equipped into the domain of the earth by supernatural means. However whilst palaeontology began in earnest in the nineteenth century it has done so coupled and encumbered with the existing state of play in political correctness. No one has been brave enough to suggest that the mind as well as the body is in a constant state of evolution. Even Darwin shied away from suggesting that Humanity is still in a state of developing evolutionary trends

Although great thinkers have pondered on the existence of consciousness and self-awareness over many centuries, there was insufficient data and other information for these essentially political philosophers to realise that they were dealing with a developing and changing mental evolution. In short the evolution of the mind.

Palaeontology has progressed vigorously in the twentieth century and whilst many mysteries remain, we have a heavily suggestive line of archaeological finds to be reasonably confident of our physical roots. There is general consensus that the first earth shaking change that set in motion the course that would lead to modern man in all his ***present forms***, was the moment when a species of great ape moved to upright bipedal form. Again there is consensus that this mighty movement took place between five and seven million years ago. For the purposes of definition, it will be convenient for the purposes of this book to use Richard Leakey's definition of 'Human' as applying to all of the known bipedal species in the archaeological trail. We will also use the word 'Homo' as the definition of the large brain species leading to modern man. We need always, when considering evolution to remember that in DNA terms the difference between a Chimpanzee and a human is only a tiny percentage. If that tiny percentage leads to the enormous differences that exist between men and chimpanzees then you can imagine infinitesimal DNA differences in the existing species of man, let us say even 00.001% will lead to quite markedly different behaviour characteristics. In all probability, genetic differences between some of the races may be larger than this.

After the first human stood upright, there was no exciting explosion of developing intellect, for it was not until a period dated around two million years ago that large brained pseudo humans or 'Homo' first appeared. At this time we also see a significant change in the physical architecture of the human skull, in that this is the first time that archaeology presents us with fully arched basicrania. This change, together with the movement of the Larynx and Pharynx was probably instrumental and certainly necessary in providing humans with a comprehensive ability to produce a wide range of sounds. Certainly without these changes we would not have been able to develop sophisticated language and communication. After this significant development, the evolution of the human is by archaeological standards greatly accelerated. Some significant developments are however still very much the subject of controversy. For instance the archaeologists are unable to agree on a common front as to when our ancestors actually began to communicate through speech. Sound leaves no fossils. It must surely be accepted as a fact however, that all humans who took part in the Great Diaspora out of Africa must have had speech ability. That fact alone, throws out the theory that the sudden flowering of art 35 thousand years ago was somehow connected with a first time ability to speak and communicate. This postulation (all of the Diaspora had speech) has to be the correct because we know that the Diaspora was largely complete some 100 thousand years ago and certainly speech could not have simply been grafted onto any non-speech populations who were already out in the wide world prior to 35000 years ago.

It is a common phenomenon in nature that when a successful species of any animal develops, it is often the case that the species produces more than one single variety of type. It is more than likely that 'adaptive radiation' took place at the human birthplace and a number of human varieties, very similar, but not essentially the same, took part in the Diaspora. It is at this point that it is fair to ask the question as to whether we have still present on earth, representatives of this 'radiation' population. We also need to remember and include in our consideration, that the Neanderthal's co-existed with Homo Sapiens for a couple of millennia. In all probability, in fact certainly, the Neanderthal's were derived from that same human radiation group that flowered 2 million years ago. Did Homo-Sapiens breed with the Neanderthal? What was the product of that breeding? We may never know. We may never know for certain, but recent revelations brought about by the use of DNA seem to have established that the Neanderthal was light skinned, red haired and as we already know, had a 10% larger brain capacity than Homo Sapiens. Is interbreeding between Homo Sapiens and the Neanderthal the solution to the inherently different nature of the ASG? Supporting this hypothesis, recent examination of a large sample of DNA from a variety of races has demonstrated that there exists in the North Western European, a gene difference associated with intellectual ability, which is not present in races from Sub Saharan Africa. The certain effects generated from this gene difference have not yet been fully established but they already clearly demonstrate that evolution is not yet ended within the human race

Incidentally, I believe that had Negro, Japanese and modern Western human skulls been found in the archaic alluvial sands of Western Tanzania, they would almost certainly have been labelled as different species.

So, we have arrived at a position in considering the ancestry of man that few argue with except in detail. From here on however I suggest developments and philosophies which are wholly new and based on the belief that evolutionary effects are not simply confined to the physical structure of our bodies but are continued in the development of the mind.

I have already illustrated the broad sweep of the Human Diaspora and now I will seek to postulate the effect that geographical isolation and isolation in time has had on the standard Human computer, the human brain or more properly the human mind. I believe the primary result of this long period of human separation is the development of various levels of intellectual consciousness, i.e. evolutionary non-physical trends, but the evolution of the mind/consciousness.

The palaeontologists have considered only the fossil record because of course, up until modern forms of communication such as writing, and the consequent recording of ideas and history, intellect had left no record. The creation of human consciousness has I believe, provided a new avenue of evolution other than the physical. I believe evolution continues with the ongoing development of the mind and that the seemingly puzzling differences in achievements that we see between the major races simply reflects the reality of the human mind evolving in different ways in different environments.

The evolution of the human mind is brought about by exactly the same mechanism, as is the physical evolutionary process. Immersed in a closed society the social needs of individuals are influenced continuously by the demands that living with others create. Minuscule changes in brain generated mind consciousness create intellectual advantages leading to social dominance. The response of the individual to these changes will be acceptable or non-acceptable in the eyes of his fellows. Long periods (thousands of years) of response observance will create auto behaviour by people involved in this long value experience. Behavioural traits will create success or failure in the particular society involved and marriages will seek to cement acceptable behavioural characteristics by husband or bride choice. The desire to conform and win admiration, or simply acceptance, are powerful forces at work in the unconscious mind and if we look closely at different racial groups we can observe quite different auto responses to common stimuli.

Again the physical environment in which a developing people are immersed is key to the progression of mind development. So the harsh unforgiving environment of the North West of Europe in the early days of settlement was a constant stimulus to evolutionary needs. It is clear that subtle variations in mind consciousness giving survival advantages are likely to have the same effect on a closed population, as do physical adaptations.

The storage of memory during life, changes the electromagnetic make-up of the human mind, it may be that some of these changes also result in inherited characteristics. Certainly artistic, musical and other creative activities are seen to pass through to descendants. We have long ago accepted that the physical pattern of our genes can be changed by response to subtle influences in our physical environment and we need to remember that physical evolutionary changes are made by natural selection of the most efficient physical response format. It is surely only a short step to accepting that the structure of the mind is subject to the same selective process.

Whilst considering the evolution of 'mind' it is not possible to ignore the effect of language structure on this evolution. Certainly a child raised exclusively with the use of say, Gaelic, as its means of communication will neither perceive nor comment on his environment in the same way as will a child of similar intelligence who is raised with English as his base communication tool. It is possible, indeed likely, that the evolution of language is part of the mechanism that the mind uses to advance. English as a tool has accompanied many of modern civilisation's advances. The depth and range of meaning, nuances and emotion generated in English can-not be repeated in any other language. Maybe this factor also contributes in some way to the failure of the Latin's with their inadequate language.

If the suggestion of evolutionary mind adaptation is true, where can we see the effect? I suggest that the evidence for this proposition is contained in quite clear evidential behaviour of different races. The most marked differences are in the management of communities. The cohesive effect of ASG evolution has produced nations who are actively seeking the projection of the good life for all its citizens. This phenomenon is not apparent in let us say Arab society. Arab social values are based around group identity rather than personal identity. The Arab nations currently creating massive problems with the organisation of international terror are reacting in the way that their societies have always reacted. These nations were among the first in mankind's history to create organised societies but no citizen of a modern day Western society would wish to have lived in any of these societies. These societies were always brutal, authoritarian, and corrupt, nothing has changed. These societies repressed personal identity and eliminated free thought. Thus it is not surprising that modern day Islam is based on a book which can not be argued with. It can not be argued with because the Arab is taught that the Koran is the irrevocable word of "God". Such an autocratic decree could not be accepted in the West, but the Arab is quite content to accept this unintelligent maxim. Notwithstanding it may be illogical and against the interest of the Islamic people, the word of the Koran can not be argued with and any who argue with it are subject to sanction. The repression of Arab freedom to think, over thousands of years even prior to the existence of the Koran has resulted in a flawed human experience that will not contribute to the future of mankind in general.

In the early twenty first century, the liberal community were enthusiastic about what they termed as the 'Arab Spring'. In this period several despotic societies experienced revolutionary social change and a number of evil dictatorships were overthrown. It must be a significant disappointment for the liberal community to find that rather than experiencing an Arab Spring the unfortunate peoples involved have simply experienced a new Arab Winter with new despotic cultures simply replacing the old ones. To anyone accepting the philosophy of this book, such a result is no surprise.

A less significant but nevertheless useful illustration is the Chinese attitude to life. For instance the attitude of a Chinese commander to troop losses compared with the average ASG commander is very different. During the Korean War the use of anti-personal mines by the allied forces was largely unsuccessful. The use of anti-personal mines has as part of its philosophy the belief that a wounded soldier will of necessity incapacitate those who will carry the wounded man to safety. This didn't happen of course in the Chinese army.

Of course ASG nations have from time to time deviated from the route to care and compassion, Nazi Germany is the extreme example of the worst form of this deviation. Nazi Germany and similar evil deviations are just that, deviations, and are soon submerged by the real route of the ASG. The Holocaust, which evil was committed by an ASG nation is the greatest recorded crime in human history.

The effect of deviations by the ASG will always be more traumatic than other nations, because of the inherent efficiency of the ASG.

It is my fundamental position that I believe that it is an unarguable reality that the human race is made up of a significant number of different levels of human evolutionary consciousness. These different levels of evolution have created the quite markedly diverse performances and behavioural patterns in the major racial divisions. It has been fashionable to suggest that these behavioural differences are due, not to inherent racial characteristics but because the failure society has not had the benefits of education and liberal social conditions. In truth of course education and liberal social organisation are themselves the products of higher achieving racial groups. These benefits are not the cause of the dominance of the ASG but are the product of the evolutionary ASG mind.

The destruction of the leading evolutionary group in our time is being speeded up because modern conditions have created a situation where it is possible to emigrate from your homeland very quickly and cheaply and this in turn means that the natural evolutionary process is being broken down. This has not occurred previously in history where large migratory movements have generally been brought about by the ambition of successful evolutionary groups acquiring slave or vassal states. Migration of the human animal in post prehistoric times has taken a number of shapes.

In the process of evolution, individual groups arise as centres of benefit i.e. the product of their achievements in organised society attract people from other evolutionary groups who have not had the same success. In historical times with limited travel capability this migration of need was necessarily slow. These migrations were generally the result of upheavals in a particular social group, leading to flight. An unusual example of this kind of forced migration is the Diaspora of the Jews following the destruction of historical Israel by the Romans. With their inherent commercial capability, the Jews fled to the then established centres of excellence such as Rome, Egypt and all centres of trade and finance in the ancient world. But here the similarity with other forced migrations changes, because the Jew was never assimilated and indeed never sought assimilation.

The Hebrew Diaspora has continued up to the present day. The Jewish people have followed power wherever it appeared, moving to Rome, Moscow, Paris, and Berlin. With the growth of British power in the seventeenth and eighteenth centuries, they made London their target and established the most powerful Jewish lobby in their history at that time eventually producing a British Prime Minister who legitimised the Zionist movement. In 1900 when the infant USA finally grew stronger than its parent Britain, the Jew began his biggest migration yet. Today the Jewish lobby in the USA is one of the most powerful human agencies on Earth. The unique experience of the Jew has created an evolutionary crèche of its own and I have placed the Jew in level one of the evolutionary table.

This form of migration in human history is unusual, because at each step, the Jew was not assimilated. Generally speaking, incoming waves of migrants are slowly assimilated into the local population leading to new gene hives and ultimately to real physical and social changes. The Jewish people have kept their gene strain relatively pure and as a consequence have not been over influenced racially by their multiple homes.

In the modern period, travel means are accessible easily and the migration of socio-economic groups seeking life improvements has been accelerated immensely. This form of migration will and is changing the world we know very rapidly and will effectively destroy the power of the West even without the coming energy crisis.

The cost of not recognising these real and important differences is unimaginably damaging. In the 21st century it probably means that the great benefits of the progress of the ASG will almost certainly be thrown away and mankind will return to the government by the uncivilised.

As the ASG disappear under the weight of different strains of evolutionary levels of the human species, in the East, the star of the Chinese race begins its ascendancy. Power without compassion will again rule humankind. Despair will be the price of multi-racialism.

Whilst considering this thesis do not for one moment expect your "other evolutionary" group friend to behave as this book suggests his racial group will behave. Racial behaviour is a group phenomenon and any individual submerged within a different evolutionary group will take on the superficial appearance and behaviour of that group. When however mass movement of a particular group changes that isolation then evolutionary behaviour will re-appear. Thus in some areas of British Northern towns any attempt to behave like the ASG is abandoned and there exists a call for Shari law. Such conglomerates of alien philosophy are mutually destructive and the host evolutionary group should move to prevent corrosion.

The cycle of a leading society being submerged by less able groups has happened through-out history, generally because the successful society or leading society at the time, enslaves or conquers a less able people and then proceeds to interbreed with this less successful stock. The result is always a diminution in the leading group capability and humanity in time will throw up a replacement, leading group. In our own time the destruction of the leading group (The ASG) is being accomplished not by conquest but by economic migration.

All human beings of whatever race are part of the same species, in the same way that a Poodle a Pekinese or an Alsatian are members of the species of dog, no-one however suggests that a Pekinese should be used as a guide dog or as a police guard dog

CHAPTER FOUR

WHO ARE THE RACES

THE NINE PRIME EVOLUTIONARY GROUPS OF MANKIND

1) **The ASG. The Jew, The British Celt.**

2) **The Latin. The Japanese. The Chinese.**

3) **The Indian. The Arab. The Korean**

4) **The Euro Asiatic.**

5) **The Indo Chinese.**

6) **The South American Indian. The Polynesian and The Inuit**

7) **The North American Indian**

8) **The Negro**

9) **The Australian Aboriginal**

NB. With the exception of level 1) this list is not fully inclusive, but simply establishes bench marks. The remainder of racial groups fit within the structure illustrated in the appropriate level.

The following is a summary of racial terms used by the writer to describe the major divisions of mankind. I identify more than nine groups because the list below includes derivative and subsidiary races with separate development from the mainstream evolutionary streams.

1) The A.S.G. These are those Europeans who's ancestral habitat is in the area North and West of a line drawn roughly from the Southerly base of the Urals and extending to the Atlantic on the southern side of Brittany. It generally excludes any peoples living historically North of Latitude 70. The term ASG is an abbreviation of the words Anglo-Scandinavian-Germanic people. The catchment area goes further South to include Austria.

2) The Latin's. These are those peoples who were primarily created by the long-term existence of the Roman Empire. They are in general the descendants of the huge slave populations together with the Romans and indigenous populations of these countries themselves. This racial group contains within it genetic ancestral trails to the ASG, North Africa, Greece, Turkey, the Saudi Peninsula and the Balkans.

3) The Arab. This ancient racial group, inhabit a huge area stretching from the Eastern Mediterranean shore to the foothills of the Hindu Kush in the East. From the Elburz Mountains in the North to Egypt in the South.

4) The Afro-Arab. This group is located in the African continent north of the Sahara and occupying the whole of the South Mediterranean Coast. They are fundamentally Arabs but with a four thousand year drip of Negro integration.

5) The Negro. This group of peoples, probably the oldest in mankind and almost certainly, the parent race of mankind, inhabit the African continent below the Sahara. This racial group is probably one of the most pure human strains with very low percentages of incoming racial blood.

6) The Indian. This racial group is located from the Suleiman Ra in the North West to the Irrawaddy in the East. From the Himalayas in the North to Ceylon in the South.

7) The Euro-Asiatic. These peoples inhabit an enormous slice of the Earth, stretching from the Black Sea in the West to the Sea of Okhotsk in the East. From the Arctic Circle in the North to the borders of China in the Southeast and the borders of Iran in the Southwest

8) The Chinese. The only single nation racial entity. Occupying the
area between the Euro-Asiatic and the Indian and extending to
The Indo-Chinese group to the South.

9) 7&8a). The Indo-Chinese. These people are the result of a joint Indian and Chinese ancestral parentage and occupy the South East Oriental archipelago. The Indian and Chinese strain is predominant in different parts of this region.

10) Australian Aboriginal. Occupying only the mainland of Australia.

11) Polynesian Peoples. Inhabit Pacific Oceana.

12) North American Indian. Occupying the continent of North America North of the Mexican deserts. Generally believed to be direct descendants of immigrants across the Bering land bridge from Asia

13) South American Indian. Occupying all of the South American continent and North America to the Mexican border. Origin unknown, but probably Asiatic

14) The Inuit Peoples. This racial group, exclusively adapted to extreme cold, generally occupies any land areas north of Latitude 70.

There are two important derivative races, which require recognition, they are: -

15) The Jewish people. This is a distinct Arab tribe, which as a consequence of world-wide dispersion, but not assimilation, is now distinctly different from other Arab peoples.

16) Korean/Japanese peoples. This small group for historical reasons is distinct from the main Chinese grouping.

There are many small derivative racial groupings around the edges of the primary groups but none with earth changing probabilities. Of course, the boundary's between these groups of peoples become fuzzy at the edges where ever there is constant contact between two groups. In general however, the racial groups identified above are recognisable both physically and behaviourally. The racial groups are the inevitable products of different environments on a common source human animal over a many million-year history.

I have not identified the current most numerous inhabitants of North America as a race in the above table because at the moment they have no universal assimilation and comprise all of the above groups to varying degrees. This is also true of the South American continent to a lesser degree.

Intermarriage between the groups identified above has inevitable consequences and the child produced by such marriages will carry obvious gene traits from both groups. Intermarriage will create a human being who will carry ***non-selective traits*** from both racial groups. The child may not fit the profile of either group and may well fall midway or lower between the rankings shown above in the characteristics used to formulate a table. Any person from a group 1 level of evolution marrying a person from any other level of evolution and producing children, will risk throwing away a million years of human development for the children who may result from such a marriage.

The destruction of a leading group is ***always*** brought about by ongoing and accelerating assimilation of subservient groups generally from different evolutionary groupings attached to the leader group by product envy. This process can be studied as it happens in the USA today.

Note, again that there is no indication that in any of the groups, basic intelligence is a factor. The differences are more closely illustrated by my previous example likening the Human brain to a basic, standard computer, which has received different software packages. Unfortunately for the human being, unlike the computer, software packages cannot be transferred from one human being to another just by plugging in a spare disc, the evolutionary experience of one group is only available to the other by genetic inheritance, and only the results of that inheritance in gene imprints are meaningful.

I say again that there is no evidence to suggest that intellectual ability in the form of cranial capacity is different in any of the racial groups. However, something that we will call **L.I.C.R.I.B.** (Lifestyle, Instincts, Collective Response and Inherited Behaviour) does divide racial groups in a very clearly observable way and provides recognisable behaviour patterns in the operation of society. L.I.C.R.I.B is the phenomena produced by differences in evolutionary consciousness. It's important here to dismiss superficial or cosmetic manifestations of difference. The phenomenon, which we are researching, is the deeply inbred result of aeons of historical experience and response. The table of evolutionary groupings are devised from a study of racial group behaviour over the entire history of man and by applying the tests of displayed emotional and cultural responses. These tests include the following:-

1) Compassion.
2) Humanitarianism.
3) Social inclusivity.
4) Social mobility.
5) Progression to social equality.
6) Progress toward educational equality.
7) Progress toward representational government.
8) Existence of personal freedom.
9) Demonstrated care for the individual

These and many other tests are those which must be applied in examining a racial group's quality of civilisation and their human ranking. The median ranking of the levels illustrated is Group Two in the evolutionary table. I.e. the Latin's. All of the other groups fail in a significant number of these tests when applied against their recent and historical profile.

The groups listed above will respond differently to common social trends wherever the local population is dominated by a particular evolutionary majority. Where individual members of a lower evolutionary level are contained and live within a higher level evolutionary group, and have no contact with their own group, their behaviour will resemble the behaviour and response of the higher evolutionary level.

CHAPTER FIVE

HOW DO THEY PERFORM

THE ASG.

This is the most successful racial group, largely responsible for the formation of what is known as the modern Western World. It is a curious fact that this group of peoples was probably the last of the Old World peoples to formulate structured society and drew heavily from the experience of the group labelled the Latin's. Whilst coming late to the table of civilisation the ASG have without exception taken the concept of personal liberty much further than their predecessors. The ASG will, where-ever they are the supreme power, build a state that is likely to be representative and will embody significant humanitarian and democratic trends. These societies may go through the cycle of Authoritarianism, Democracy, extreme Liberalism, Tyranny and back to Democracy several times in its history, but the trend will always be toward a more humane society.

That which in the beginning of the twenty-first century has been recognised, as 'Western Civilisation' is in reality the sum of the experience of the ASG over the last 2000 years. This experience has created the most beneficial and successful societies in history. Ordinary people living within these societies enjoy a standard of living unknown even to kings in previous societies.

None of the other primary racial groups has produced or even successfully borrowed and implemented the life style conditions of the ASG.

It is necessary here to deal with the legend of Greek pre-eminence in the matter of representative democracy. Academics and the politically correct like to claim that what we call Western democracy is a direct result of the limited experiments in limited democracy witnessed in Greece at around the time of Pericles. The reality of course is that the trade union movement in the UK, the fledgling struggle in Germany, Great Britain and other ASG countries toward democracy, was a movement arising strictly out of the experience of the ASG. None of the authors of these movements would have been able to point to Greece on the map, let alone quote the age of Pericles as an example. The robber barons who wrung the Magna Carta out of an unwilling King were simply reacting to their own needs. Philosophers of the time had not yet resurrected the unhealthy legend of Greek democracy.

Under the weight of frenetic multi-racialism, these, the ASG societies, the most successful societies in history are already engaged in a process, which will if unchecked lead to their destruction and eventual extinction.

The process of destruction is the simple process of racial assimilation, where the successful members of the racial groups who are members of the ASG, are willingly allowing the members of lower value societies from different levels of evolution to blend their genes. The result, as in every case of cross-evolutionary level blending, is the lowering of the higher order of evolutionary development and the raising of the lower order of evolutionary development.

Who are the peoples of the ASG? They are those people who have inherited the genes of the races historically inhabiting the following countries. England, Germany, Norway, Sweden, Denmark, Holland, Finland, Austria, Czech Republic, Poland, Lithuania, Latvia. There is of course a huge ASG population in the USA and Canada. The L.I.C.R.I.B. of the ASG has created those societies, which all men seek to enjoy.

The source of the racial group I have labeled the ASG seems to have been in North Central Europe, with population growth pushing continuous movement westward. The movement of this mighty group was a long drawn out event over the best part of 20,000 years, it continued until its final stage, the settlement of the country we now call England.

Isolation does, as we will see in the case of China, produce maverick results and it is obvious that the rate of human evolutionary development is much faster than other animals; this is probably because to some degree the human is himself a manipulator of his own environment. A phenomenon of this process is the country and people of England. The people of England and the recognisable country that we call England today were born on the 14th October 1066. In the five and a half preceding centuries to that date the indigenous Celts had been driven out of the lowlands of the British Isles into Wales and Scotland and their places taken by successive waves of invaders from North Western Europe. All of these invaders came from the same racial and geographical stock with similar languages and cultures. All of these invaders were from ASG tribes. The Celts who were driven out were a people who preceded the ASG invasions and had been part of the settlement of South Western Europe prior to the Roman creation of the Latin. The Roman's, whilst occupying and administering Britain for almost 350 years did not seriously colonise. The Roman villa's and other town ruins found in profusion in England are generally speaking, the abode of Romanised locals. Similarly the Roman legions generally served a short part of their army life in Britain and then returned to sunnier climes. Some settlements did take place of course, but not in significant numbers.

It is historical lunacy to describe the peoples of the British Isle's before the ASG invasions as having anything in common with the people we today call English, although the descendants of those who came before the English still live in Wales and Scotland. Similarly, we need to understand that the Norman invasion of England was not an invasion by the French. William the Conqueror regarded the French as foreigners and as enemies. William the Conqueror was himself the grandson of a Viking rover and the people of Normandy were so called because the Norsemen had settled this area of Northern France. They were in fact, the same source people who had already settled in the British Isles. William had, incidentally, as a matter of record, common ancestry with Edward the Confessor and King Cnut. Thus we are not talking about a Latin invasion of the British Isles but simply a redistribution of land among Norse warriors. In any case, as in the example of the Roman's, the Norman's never carried out a large-scale colonisation of England. Their fortress occupation was supported by a few foreign Norman troops at first, but quickly local armies were recruited from the shires.

The maturity of the nation that developed from that date in 1066 and the conflict at Hastings is extraordinary, one of history's miracles. With a relatively small landmass and a population, which did not reach ten million until the beginning of the nineteenth century, the country that grew out of that battle was to have a greater effect on the history of the world than has any other nation so far. In those same centuries, as England grew in power and influence, the region of Normandy from whence the Conqueror came, was absorbed into the racial anonymity of the French and would play no further independent role in the history of the world.

From that day in 1066, England existed in physical geographical isolation whilst enjoying full access to the streams of political and cultural thinking deriving from the rest of the world. Whilst armies came and went over the surface of Europe scattering the gene banks of the various peoples indiscriminately across a dozen nations. England enjoyed the long peace of a thousand years, broken only by civil war. The gene hive of the English flourished in that long peace and the people who resulted were inventive, creative, curious and militarily, incredibly successful. The language of these people would become the linga-franca of the world and the nations, which were founded by this people, the most desired places to live on Earth. Located as it is, in one of the stormiest areas of the oceans, English sailors, of necessity became the masters of the art of navigation and seamanship. This expertise gave them mastery of the Oceans and Seas. During this time the Union of Scotland and Wales which created Britain, added a new dimension to the British table of abilities.

The beginning of industrialisation in Britain is no accident but the result of a thousand year settled order with the opportunity for the maturation of scholarship and education. But truly the incredible success of this small country would lead one to say, if in the last two hundred years, you sought to label any people as the super-race, that race would be the British. There is **never** of course a 'super race' the sifting of the human gene bank will create new centres of excellence on a continuous basis. ***Note what I say you politically correct, there is never a 'super race' only a currently dominant race.***

This extraordinary history is now threatened with extinction, not brought about by violent attack but by socio-economic immigration. Immigration into the UK is largely made up of level 3, 5 and 8 evolutionary groups. The behaviour characteristics of these groups are now common in the UK. Take the City of London as an example, if you make a simple chart of immigrant settlement figures into the UK and similarly chart the immigrant related serious crime, street violence, rape, murder and gun crime, there is a clear relationship between the two sets of statistics

THE LATINS

This name which is already widely used, I have applied to the second most successful human group in history. In genetic makeup the Latin is a leftover from the Roman Empire, the people who make up this group are the descendants of the huge slave populations of the Roman Empire plus the indigenous Celtic and Gaelic tribes who inhabited this region prior to the rise of Rome. Whilst I have included Spain in this group, residual genetic material from the Afro-Arab is strongly present in Central and Southern Spain as a result of the occupation of large areas of Spain by the Moors

The Latin has contributed greatly to all forms of Art, Architecture and spiritual ethos. Despite this wonderful contribution the Latin demonstrates his restricted level of evolution when placed in a position of administrative power of land and people. The best and most striking illustration of this failure is the example laid out clearly for us on the American continent.

One of the great natural tragedies for the peoples of Earth was the Latin discovery of the Americas. The arrival of Columbus doomed the South American continent. As a result of the Latin discovery and their subsequent colonisation of South America, the existing peoples of that continent, who themselves had already generated some of the least attractive societies in human history found themselves administered by yet another failed society. As a result of that colonisation, these peoples were subjected to the standard level of Latin incompetence and the societies that have emerged in this great continent have created misery and social chaos to disfigure the society of man. This continent which should have been a great provider of wealth and security for the peoples of Earth has become a byword for sloth and corruption.

Draw a straight line on the American continent where the US/Mexican border is located. Contrast the civilisations that exist north of that line with those that exist south of that line. North of the line, are two mighty nations Canada and the USA, whose populations enjoy the highest levels of civilisation. To the South of that line a collection of countries with varying levels of despair and poverty and human degradation as a daily diet. Yet all of the geographical topography of the terrain north of the line, exists to the south of the line. Why then are the Northern nations successful and the Southern countries are largely failures? The answer of course, is that those nations north of the line, were colonised by the ASG led by the British and those countries to the south of the line were colonised by the Spanish and Portuguese. In my table of evolutionary values, the Latin's are only one step behind the ASG, yet observe what a difference that one step makes in the colonisation of a continent.

Let us suppose that we could go back in history by just four hundred years and arrange that the modern day country of Brazil could be colonised by the British and settlement of this land be denied to the Portuguese. What would be the modern day result?

Imagine for a moment the country of Brazil. A gigantic country of 3.286.487 square miles, a country laden with all the natural riches that nature can endow. Brazil has a population of some 185 million people (last census, probably inaccurate to 50 million people) and was settled by the Portuguese. In the council of nations, Brazil's voice is a whisper in the anteroom. Brazil has extremes of wealth and poverty and a huge underclass of rootless half-starved people who look on enviously through the windows of the wealthy. The country infrastructure is chaotic and its social services and people care exist in rudimentary form only.

Now in our imaginary time travel we have changed that reality and this country has been colonised by the British. With its enormous resources and huge geographical extent added to the dynamic power of the ASG can there be any doubt that that country would have soon become one of the most powerful nations on earth? Taking its place beside Australia, Canada, New Zealand and the USA in the list of desirable places to live.

This suggested difference is simply the result of the Latin overlord of South America being just one level of evolution behind the Anglo Saxon settlers of North America.

Since this paragraph was written in 2003 Brazil has discovered its enormous natural resources and is posing on the world as a new super power in international wealth. This newly discovered power will do nothing for the poor and dispossessed of Brazil but will accentuate the difference between rich and poor in that country.

The failure of Latin America is written in extremes of poverty, millions live below any measure of subsistence. Millions are affected daily by the passage of guerrilla wars, national leaders are replaced on a dreary roundabout of place seeking, each one as bad as they whom they replace.

Unlike British colonialism, the Spanish and Portuguese, when they were driven out of South America, left no social infrastructure, simply a collection of places existing only as names on a map. This was the legacy of all Latin colonisation throughout the world, in Africa, in the Middle and Far East and in the Islands. Nowhere has an ex Latin colony become a place of world significance. This is not an accident; this is the reality of race and evolution. Contrast Macao and Hong Kong, Macao a filthy decaying backwater, Hong Kong, a dynamic world economic reality. The difference in geography? Nil. The difference in colonisation? Hong Kong colonised by the British and Macao by the Portuguese.

The group mind of the Latin or its L.I.C.R.I.B is what its evolutionary level provides and no Latin can escape that condition. Wherever tested the Latin will fail where the ASG will succeed.

FRANCE

Of all the Latin nations, France fails a level one evolutionary grading by two tests only.

France has been the most successful of this second level evolutionary group but nevertheless betrays many of the weaknesses of that group. France's role in Europe in modern times has generally been destructive. The French revolution in the late eighteenth century was plastered with all the most desirable of human platitudes, Equality, Fraternity & Liberty. As usual with the French, the rhetoric was more able than the reality. Instead of liberty the French were thrust into a brutal military dictatorship, instead of fraternity the French set about the extermination of thousands of their European colleagues. Instead of equality the French sought economic and military repression of Europe. Later on, French behaviour during the reign of Napoleon 111 in the later part of the nineteenth century created many of the basic elements that created the First World War. French unprincipled ambition in the Eastern Mediterranean during the decline of the Ottoman Empire destabilised that region and left many sores that came back to haunt Europe.

In Europe at this present time France will ensure the long-term failure of the EU. She will do so by the pursuit of totally selfish policies. When France considers any matter of world affairs, she does so only on the basis of is it good for France and will embrace any action that affirms that question even if the action undertaken is against the interests of the rest of humanity. France never considers any co-operation unless it fulfils the entirely selfish requirement of French interests first, even at the expense of the rest of the world.

France will happily sign any international agreement but will in fact only honour those perceived to fulfil its own selfish need. We will rarely hear any objection from the French on any criteria of EU policy but whether the criteria will be implemented in France is entirely another matter. In international politics France cannot be trusted in any circumstances. France honestly believes that Britain with its culture of strict adherence to any international agreement signed; even when not in the best interests of Britain is insane. France is totally and culturally unable to understand the concept of international honour. France only understands manipulative and acquisitive politics.

The French as colonial overlords carried their self-concern to extremes, there are no examples of ex French colonial territories prospering after independence. This failure is simple the consequence of the French belief that to spend money on anything in a colonial territory which did not immediately profit continental France was unnecessary. They left behind no infrastructure or national regeneration plan; rarely did they leave any sense of nationhood. France can never be trusted with the administration of a colonial territory.

At the end of the Napoleonic wars, Britain was in possession of most of France's colonial territories. Incredibly and sadly for the world Britain returned these colonies to France.

France is also hampered in the support of international polices by Her hatred of the Anglo- Saxon. Notwithstanding the fact that French liberty is entirely the consequence of Anglo Saxon deliverance in two world wars, the French see Britain and the USA as the enemy of France.

THE ARAB

The Arab is a progenitor of European civilisation, being one of the_first human groups to create leisure and organised society, this arising from the creation of wealth which in turn was derived from the discovery and exploitation of agriculture and husbandry. In India and China at the same time that this phenomenon was occurring, exactly similar developments were taking place. Civilisations across the Arab area of influence grew to majestic levels and communication in the form of writing, exchange mechanism's in the form of currency and financial structures in the form of taxation and national budgets all made their appearance at this time. Mighty nations and Empires came and went in the five millennia that this group held sway among humankind. Each of these mighty expressions of mankind's ingenuity expressed the awesome capabilities of the human mind, in Architecture, engineering, military organisation, hierarchical social structure, administration and everything to do with the organisation of a state.

Despite this extraordinary merit, each of these Nations and Empire's lacked the essential quality of compassion or even the suggestion of personal freedom. These were essentially slave states, where even the ordinary citizen as opposed to a captured slave, existed in servitude to the state or Tyrant currently in power. The essential nature of this people has not changed and in any situation where the Arab is pre-eminent in the exercise of power, then that state is likely to be corrupt, brutal and unrepresentative of the individual. Such states will be inefficient and exploitive and will not provide the requirements of a civilised life to its ordinary citizens.

The continuing daily frenzy of the Arab nations is a source of incredulity for most western citizens. The continuing horror of murder and bestial behaviour almost mind numbing in its endless continuum.

If we listen to the television reporters or read the Liberal editorials we will discover to our surprise that these horrific events are never the fault of the killers or the victims but the responsibility of us in the West. Somehow we have failed to give leadership or money or guidance or whatever to these poor unfortunates who roam the streets of far away places killing all and sundry and without regard to guilt or innocence. It is our failure to respect Islam that has turned this religion into a haven for psychotics and inhuman killers.

Of course all of this is arrant nonsense.

The awful events we see unfold on our screens is simply a modern continuum of the kind of behaviour that these evolutionary groups have always engaged in. And what is true of the Arab is true of the other evolutionary groups. ***It is not possible to act as a nation outside the bounds of your evolutionary experience.***

The current and developing perception that Islam is evil and leading its people into horrific acts is inaccurate. It is the Arab people that are the problem, not their religion. If they didn't have Islam they would have some other unifying evil to identify with. All of their historic civilisations have been oppressive and cruel.

The Arab today is at the same evolutionary level as when as a people they first appeared on the world stage. They look at the west of the ASG and are genuinely puzzled by our humanism. To the Arab this humanism is simply weakness. Politicians in the West are obsessed with changing these awful societies by example and exhortation, it can not be done, only the passage of centuries in a controlled environment will achieve real environmental change. The evidence that otherwise the past will be endlessly repeated is all around us in the pages of recent and distant history. The evolutionary condition of a people does not change overnight; it can take many many years to achieve real change. This is true of all peoples, not simply the Arab.

For instance the massacre in Tienaman Square has been repeated in China's history more times than we could possibly count. It will happen again.

The awful brutality of the Japanese invasion of China where the deliberate and unprovoked killing of millions of Chinese went on as an act of policy is not new. Japan has treated its enemies in this way for all of its recorded history. Japan will do it again. Do not be deceived by the gentle face that Japan is currently showing to the world, it is only a charade.

The truth is that leopards do not change their spots, they remain leopards and carnivores and killers and you may never turn them into domesticated cats. Just when you think the lion is tamed he will catch you unawares and you will die. Unfortunately this is also true of the different levels of human evolution. They do not change their spots either and we can predict their forward behaviour based on their history.

THE INDIAN

The Indian Sub Continent in the Indus Valley was one of four primary sites, which produced the earliest civilisations. Starting from their central African place of origin we are now fairly sure that Homo Sapiens had arrived in all regions of the globe except Oceana sometime around 20,000 years BC. However, early human remains dating from 100,000 years ago have been found in China. Therefore the Indian subcontinent on route from the migration out of Africa was almost certainly populated long before the Harappan happening. It is clear that the Indus valley was urbanised very early on (circa 3000 BC) and flowered with the Harappan civilisation. This short-lived civilisation was probably preceded by two to three millennium of urban development. This civilisation (Harappan. 2600-1900BC) is roughly a contemporary of the Egyptian Pre Dynastic and perhaps two millennium after the Sumerian civilisation. (4500-1900BC) China's urban development began roughly simultaneously with the Sumerian. (Perhaps 1000 years earlier). Note that all of these dates are approximate only. There is no evidence of more than transitory communication between the first civilisations. There is no evidence that one of these primordial societies exported its knowledge and helped in developing new societies. The evidence suggests that in any human congregation where population reaches a point where the development of agriculture is essential to support further growth, then society develops.

There is a continuous line of civilised development in India commencing with the Harappan (although that particular civilisation was over-run in extreme violence after only a comparatively short period) and extending through to the English conquest. Examinations of these various phases show continuous growth in most of the *trappings* of civilisation, Architecture, Military organisation, Hierarchical social structure, but no indication of continuous movement toward Indian sub-continent unity or any movement toward those conditions which we recognise as bestowing universally the modern concept of human rights.

Only the Gupta Empire (320-550 AD) came close to uniting India and that in itself was a short run phenomenon. India was not a single administrative unit until forced to be so by the British. In fact India as a discrete whole did not exist until the British created it. Nor were the disparate sections of India considered as a nation until nominated as such by the British.

India throughout its history exhibits all of the contradictions of tantalising progress in material culture and negative development of personal liberty. This is stranger still when one considers that India has continued to produce throughout its history, religious revolutions that initially sought to establish personal liberties as a right. India in the 500 years before the British conquest was stuck in an unchanging sterile structured society, which offered no hope to the individual.

Both historical India and Pakistan are failed civilisations if judged on the values of compassion and humanity. If you ask an Indian, he will say their failure was a result of the British occupation. The Indian will ignore the incompetent society that preceded the British. If you ask how such a small country as the UK could overwhelm a sub-continent, all sorts of non-responsibility reasons will emerge. The truth of course is that the Indian continent (There was no Indian nation) was full of corruption and divided by a rigid caste system. Officials could be bought and sub-continent armies reflected these divisions and were easy meat for the British. It is worth remembering that gunpowder was being used in India long before it appeared in Western Europe. When the British took India there was no disparity in armament available and Indian numbers should have guaranteed success.

Britain administered India with a small occupying army and the presence of very few British personnel. Many Mr. and Mrs Smith's, civil servants, invisible in England, sat at the top of a wholly Indian pyramid of administration and policed sections of India sometimes bigger than Wales. These invisible and forgotten Mr. and Mrs Smith's did more for the wellbeing of India than all the modern aid agencies on earth. They would, after a lifetime's service in India return to live out their lives on a civil service pension in rural England. The administration was equable and wise and India in this period developed a single state civil service that stood India in good stead after independence. An objective examination of British time in India would conclude that British rule in India was probably the best example in history of the benevolent administration of conquered territory.

It has become fashionable to castigate the role of the British in India but the reality is that this period in India, the Raj, was probably the most outstanding example in the entire history of the world of a people administered by an occupying force. India was no more exploited than is any supplier of goods by the buyer.

British occupation took a sub-continent made up of many kingdoms and serfdom's. The occupation created and united in peace one of the worlds largest countries, created a civil service that is still functioning, united the geographical area of India with railroads that still run and built a basic democracy which is perhaps the most successful example of such a society outside the ASG.

CHINA

One of the first three human groups to produce recognisable civilisations, this race was isolated from Western world influences to a much more exaggerated degree than any other group. This isolation has produced a race, which is markedly different in almost every facet than the rest of the world. This race is alien in its thoughts and philosophy and the societies that this race has created throughout the long centuries are all devoid of compassion. The Chinese anthill, with its worker and soldier ants, presents the greatest danger to civilisation, as we know it.

The Chinese economy will be the most powerful on earth in the 2020's and militarily the Chinese will surpass the combined resources of the West before the century is half over. China has little oil and when the worldwide shortage of fossil fuels starts to bite in the '60's and seventies of this century China will move to protect her supplies. China will not behave, as we would expect a Western nation to behave, she will use whatever is necessary to secure the lubrication of life. In that coming conflict the West will not be safe from either atomic or biological weapons. To the Chinese mentality it would be foolish to refrain from the use of your most potent weapons in a war of survival. China has always been prepared to sacrifice millions of her own people in her struggles and will do so again. The first contest for oil resource will probably be between the Japanese and China over the control of those supplies in the Sea of Japan. The conflict over this resource will also be the first demonstration of the inability of the USA to influence world events.

The USA will have to choose between allowing the subjugation of Japan or world war three commencing with an attack on China. With the possibility of losing millions of its own people the USA will not risk confrontation with China. Unfortunately for the people of the World, China is becoming the world manufacturing superpower as the West declines and will soon have a military arsenal which will rival the USA in every department.

Incidentally, the beginnings of this coming rivalry between China and Japan are already leading to an embryonic rearmament movement in Japan. Japan has the means to create a military structure as effective as any in the world. We have recent experience of Japan as a world class military power. It was not a pleasant experience.

Neil Armstrong was the first man to stand upon the Moon but most of those who follow in the great adventure in space are likely to be Chinese unless the ASG recognises its historic mission.

CHAPTER SIX

THE FAILURE OF THE NEGRO

Note added December 2016. This chapter was written in 2003, so, for instance Nelson Mandela was still alive. Interestingly the forecast that I made on the progress of South Africa after his death which is currently descending into financial chaos are remarkably accurate.

The Negro in his insulated cockpit of sub Saharan Africa lived for 2 millions of years in a relatively unchanging environment. For evolution to work, the existing conditions need to be challenged and in this period of history no challenge existed. There was virtually no contact with the world developing around the Mediterranean. The Negro remained what he had been since Homo emerged. He was a hunter-gatherer, he did not develop the wheel, he built no ships nor even developed the bow and arrow. His fierce, immoral and warlike mien did not change at all in the two millennia. Whilst printing and art flourished and architecture built the Taj-Mahal and Salisbury Cathedral North of the Sahara, in the land of the Negro the endless days of live, eat and kill went on and on and on. Let us look how the Negro has behaved since exposed to the rest of the world. The following examination does not contain all of the countries below the Sahara but is certainly representative of that dark and sad continent. I have also included Haiti from the West Indies because as most people will know Haiti was the first of the modern Negro republics. Some of the countries not included have even worst records than those listed below.

Haiti

This unfortunate land was discovered by Columbus in 1492, taken over by the French in 1697 and became the first independent Negro republic in 1804. The island paradise found by Columbus carried with it all of the promise of the New World, and indeed whilst in the possession of the French (1697.) was one of the richest economies in the Caribbean. Following the take-over by the Negro slaves the island has become a byword for degradation and evil. Life on this island has become a hell on earth and violent death an ever-present reality. Life expectation is just 53 years and quality of life almost totally absent. This is one of the poorest countries in the Western world. Everything that is bad about human society is commonplace in Haiti. Haiti today is a reminder what incompetent and immoral government can do to the earthly paradise.

Angola

Angola became independent from Portugal in 1975 and immediately began a twenty-seven-year civil war, millions of people were displaced from their homes and upward of a million and a quarter were killed. Typically for a Latin colonial power, the Portuguese left no meaningful infrastructure or civil service. Since independence the country has engaged in the destruction of its own biodiversity by poor farming and forestry practice. The country has significant reserves of oil and diamonds. Currently there is no real stability within the country and civil war is likely to break out again at any time. This country is a drain on the world aid programme with no demonstrable gain to its impoverished people. A typical African social failure.

Burkina

Gained independence from France in 1960. Throughout the '70s and 80's a series of military coups destabilised the country. Inadequate land management means overgrazing and consequent soil impoverishment. Burkina is one of the poorest countries in the world and in real terms has no prospect of altering that situation as an independent country. High-density population, high level of HIV, significant Muslim presence (50%) lead to an average life expectancy of 48 years.

Benin

Gained independence from France in 1960. Following a series of military dictatorships elected a Marxist government, which further impoverished the country. Benin has a subsistence economy. Relatively peaceful at the moment the country has no real financial or humanitarian future.

Republic of Congo

Gained independence from France in 1960 and endured 25 years of Marxist government. A civil war in 1997 led to constant ethnic unrest and there is an existing humanitarian crisis of significant proportions at this time. The country is a humanitarian disaster. This country has significant oil resource and should be wealthy and stable

Democratic Republic of Congo

This country received its independence from Belgium in 1960 and immediately plunged into a series of violent governmental changes. The rise of Joseph Mabuto brought violence and terror on an enormous scale and the consequences of that presence are still being felt. Millions have died violently in this country since independence and the sad reality is that many more will die in the near future. This country has enormous natural resources and should be one of the world's richest nations. Were it to be administered by an ASG government it would rapidly become the most powerful nation in Africa.

Guinea

Gained independence from France in 1958. Has experienced the dreary inevitability of the military seizing power in 1984 and indeed no democratic election were held until 1993. Guinea is in a state of permanent humanitarian disaster although it possesses significant natural resources and should be one of the more prosperous of Africa's nations. 40% of the people live below the poverty line and life expectation is short.

Ghana

This was the first of Britain's African colonies to achieve independence. There were high hopes for this country in 1957. N'krumah the first President spoke eloquently of freedom and prosperity. His autocratic rule brought neither to his country. This country, which was left with a sophisticated civil service and infrastructure when the British left and which had considerable natural resources is another example of the African Negro's inability to manage human affairs. Ghana has felt all the effects of military coups, dictatorships, pseudo democratic elections etc. The country is legendary for its level of corruption only rivalled by Nigeria in this context. A wonderful piece of Geography destroyed by its people. The Tax payers of the West are pleased no doubt that their hard earned resources given in loans to this country has largely been written off.

CHAD

Chad was a French possession until 1960. Typically, when the French left there remained no suggestion of a structured country or civil service. As the French left, Chad fell immediately into continuous civil war, which cost hundreds of thousands Chadians their lives and destroyed what primitive infrastructure remained after the French left. This civil war lasted for thirty years. In 1996 elections were held and again in 2001. These elections were a mockery of true democratic process and have accomplished little. 80% of the population live below the poverty line. Chad is a huge recipient of money aid, but the ordinary people of Chad see little of what is received. Chad is a human disaster.

Central African Republic.

The Central African Republic was a French colony until 1960. As the French left, the country collapsed into lawlessness and in 1972 produced one of the worst madmen of many that Africa has so far produced. Bokassa took power in a military coup and ran the country as a military dictatorship. Human rights, vestigial in any case, simply disappeared. Bokassa crowned himself Emperor in 1977 believing he was a reincarnation of Napoleon Bonaparte. In a country whose people live continuously below the poverty line, Bokassa built the largest personal palace in Africa. He has been accused of horrific crimes including cannibalism and was at one time sentenced to death for many murders of political opponents. The Central African Republic is a typical African place of human despair.

KENYA

Kenya as a British colony was extremely successful. Independence from the UK was achieved in 1963.Agriculture in the hands of white settlers made Kenya a net exporter of foodstuffs and the average Kenyan citizen was on the way to a structured society with growing standards of living. From 1969 until 1982 Kenya was a one party state and Kenyan prosperity declined continuously. Kenya has an infamous reputation for corruption at all levels of government and in all branches of the civil service. 50% of the population now live below the poverty line and inter tribal squabbling means that no clear path forward exists. If you travel to Mombassa and

stay in a hotel you will probably be surrounded by barbed wire with armed guards patrolling for your safety. Present day Kenya is an example of what Negro administration can do to a near ideal geographical package. The international community as a consequence of perceived corruption has routinely withdrawn aid packages. The present administration elected on an anti corruption platform is now itself (2006) shown to be involved in corrupt practice.
Kenya to those who knew it before independence is a sad reflection on wasted opportunities.

IVORY COAST

The Ivory Coast received independence from France in 1960. This country demonstrates the now familiar pattern of deterioration with military coups in 1999 and failed coup in 2002. Competing groups divide the country and peace is only maintained by the presence of French troops. The country had very large natural resources that have not secured the prosperity of the people, 37% of whom live below the poverty line. Aids is present as a 7% portion of the population and life expectancy is only 48 years. Typically failed Negro government with rampant corruption and the rapid destruction of the ecosystem by enormous deforestation.

LIBERIA

This country benefited from the introduction of freed American slaves and has theoretically a legal system based on Anglo/ American jurisprudence. However in its long history it has simply demonstrated on a continuous basis the Negro inability to govern. Years of civil war have decimated the country and life expectancy is 38 years only. The current situation inside the country is volatile and inherently unstable. A no hope experiment that started out with such high expectations.

Mozambique

A Portuguese colony until 1975 this country fell into a murderous civil war as soon as the Portuguese left. This awful brutal and ferocious war continued until 1992 and devastated the country's resources. International loans have been written off but it remains to be seen whether this will make any long term difference. Life expectancy is 40 years and aids is present in 12.2% of the population. The banking system is bedevilled with large-scale corruption. Most of the population works in subsistence agriculture.

NIGER

Gained independence from France in 1960, fell immediately into a one party state. In 1993 the first of a number of military coups continued the decline of the country's economy. This is one of the poorest countries in the world and there would appear little hope that it has the ability to change that reality. All the ecological evils are present with deforestation and overgrazing together with the elimination of rare wildlife species.

NIGERIA

Nigeria became independent from the UK in 1960. The British left a country which had a well-developed civil service and which was a net food exporter. The country has very large oil deposits and many other natural resources. Today Nigeria is a net importer of food and an economy which has constantly to be bailed out by the international community. Nigerian corruption is legendary and probably the worst in a continent where corruption is endemic. Nigeria has of course endured a brutal civil war with many deaths and has routinely experienced all the consequences of incompetent government. This country should have been the Star of African independence; instead it is a place where you only go if you have to.

TOGO

Became independent from France in 1960 and plunged immediately into military rule, which has lasted until 2005. Major human rights abuses and political unrest mean that this country has not yet had any opportunity to deal with the prospect of real government. This country can only make headway with the construction of proper democratic institutions and help from the international community. Togo is simply a desperate human failure.

UGANDA

Britain gave Uganda independence in 1962. This beautiful fertile country with adequate rainfall and a climate, which means that in some areas two crops a year can be harvested, should be one of the desired places to live in the world. Yet since independence, Uganda has plumbed the bottom of the horrors of Africa. The rule of Idi Amin (1971-1979) was an eight-year nightmare in which 300,000 people were murdered. In that time the total collapse of the economy increased the people's misery. Idi Amin was thrown out finally and then replaced by yet another horror story. The reign of Milton Obote was accompanied by another 100,000 deaths. The wonderful biodiversity of Uganda is currently being destroyed by over grazing and deforestation. Poachers' roam the country killing endangered species without hindrance and ethnic fighting continues unabated. With high levels of aids and corruption at all levels of government Uganda's future is dark indeed.

ZAMBIA

Zambia became independent from Britain in 1964 and within the usual short period fell into one party rule. The country has gone through supposed democratic election process but violations, intimidation and unrest have accompanied each election. Zambia has large mineral deposits and having returned some of these to private management is again earning revenue. However the country has an endemic aids problem with some 17% of the population declared as sufferers. Widespread and unchecked poaching is threatening the very existence of elephant, rhino and all of the big cats. Deforestation and subsistence overgrazing are also contributing to an ecological disaster.

The Zambian people are locked into the cycle of African mismanagement and have no real prospect of escaping it.

ZIMBABWE

One time Rhodesia finally became independent from Britain in 1980 following a period of rule by the resident white population. The white minority government had declared unilateral independence in 1965. Under minority white rule the then Rhodesia was on the path to real success but subject to sanctions the regime could not survive. On independence in 1980 the country was renamed Zimbabwe and Robert Mugabe elected to power. Mugabe emerged as the typical African madman and the decline of the country began. Rhodesia was a fertile and productive country under both Britain and the government of Ian Smith. A net exporter of food and an infrastructure as good as anything in Africa. The country is now on the edge of starvation and all commodities are in short supply. Mugabe's insane redistribution of land away from the efficient white to illiterate Negro's destroyed the agricultural basis of Zimbabwe's economy. Zimbabwe is now an international pariah and only a brutal police and army system maintains Mugabe in power. The people of Zimbabwe are locked into a continuing horror story.

THE UNION OF SOUTH AFRICA

This rich and fertile country received its independence from Britain in 1931 and until the '90s was governed by the minority white population. In this time South Africa was extremely successful with European style infrastructure and facilities. The white administrators of this beautiful land had built a thriving financial sector, and a continuous growth in medical and service structures. Well farmed food output fed the surrounding areas of Africa. Apartheid applied with no program of structured advancement of the Negro however led South Africa into conflict with the rest of the Western world and ultimately brought about the end of white rule. However there is still an influential white minority (almost 10% of the population) which means that South Africa has continued to function with some success. There is however a constant flight from South Africa by the remaining white population and the future success depends on a number of factors. The death of Nelson Mandela is pivotal to the future of South Africa, there are already signs within the present structure of South Africa's government which give concern about the future direction of policy. If subsequent to Mandela's death the government moves toward land redistribution away from the efficient white's to the Negro, then the country will go the way of all the other African countries. The white flight from South Africa will become a flood and the economy will go down the drain. There are already pressures within South Africa for land redistribution and without the steady hand of Nelson Mandela behind the scenes, and then those pressures will increase. There are significant tribal differences within the Union and these have the capacity to raise the spectre of civil strife in the future. As long as land distribution remains as it is and as long as the white population remain, South Africa has a chance to succeed, change either of those factors and South Africa will become the greatest funeral pyre in Africa.

NB. Note added in 2016. The once leading economy of South Africa has now reached the state of 'Junk Bonds'. Fear for the future of this country.

Conclusion

The above examination of the dreadful societies created by the Negro people of Africa since colonialism leads inevitably to a number of important conclusions:-

The Negro stands clearly revealed as a race incapable of good government. Any population exposed to majority Negro administration will experience institutionalised evil at every facet of life. ***No self engendered Negro society has ever in history been a success or created social conditions anywhere approaching anything we could label civilised.*** Those liberals who campaigned vigorously for an end to the colonial administration of Africa should be made aware that they have subscribed directly to the deaths of many millions of innocent African's killed in acts of genocide and starvation brought about by continuous civil wars, wars fought without principle. How people like Peter Hain can sleep at night with the deaths of millions of Africans directly attributable to the causes he has supported is difficult to understand.

There can be no doubt that had the colonial authorities resisted the 'Wind of Change' many millions of Africans who lie in unmarked graves as victims of ethnic cleansing or simple murder would still be alive today. In addition Sub Saharan Africa would by now have been moving toward full literacy and possessed of an infrastructure and civil service which might be producing the kind of society that the ASG demand as a right. The colonial areas administered by the British would now have had among them, economies that would measure with the best in the world.

Instead Sub Saharan Africa is a sterile desert, a monument to African incompetence.

An interesting statistic is that following decolonisation, those administrations left behind by Latin colonial powers, generally collapsed into anarchy within twelve months. Country's which were left behind by British administrators in Africa collapsed into anarchy in about five years on average.

The lesson of Africa is twofold; firstly it re-illustrates the effect created by level one and two evolutionary powers (British and Latin) on a subject people. We have covered this fully in our previous chapter and secondly it illustrates the absolute reality of the failure of the Negro to absorb the experience of either level one or two evolutionary societies. Any Negro can fulfil any role in society provided he is embedded in an ASG or other higher level evolutionary population and subject to its rules. Wherever the Negro is in majority be it government, army, police or industry, that body will fail.

ASG administration will often paste a thin veneer of civilised behaviour over otherwise awful societies. It does not take much to illustrate how thin that veneer is when some natural catastrophe threatens. Watching looters and rapists in the deprived black areas of the devastated city of New Orleans after Hurricane Katrina should surprise no one. Remove the effective law and order imposed by the ASG on any Negro population and the same result will ensue. The underclass Negro in that city simply reverted to type as soon as ASG law collapsed.

The failure of the Negro has not only been deadly for the human population of Africa but has also been a disaster of epic proportions for the rare wildlife of this continent. Sub Saharan Africa contains many of the rarest species of wild life on the planet. They are all of them threatened by the absolute indifference to their fate which most African governments display.

What happened in fact was that in the three millennia of prehistory and human development played out in the rest of the world. In Africa the needle of human development stuck and the Negro endlessly played out his horrific pantomime of hunter killer life until rescued by the arrival of the Europeans in the seventeenth century.

Those who for whatever reason campaigned for an end to the colonisation of Africa, created in the final analysis one of the greatest tragedy's to befall mankind. Since decolonisation, millions of Africans have died in the most horrific circumstances. The death toll is probably four times as high as the Jewish holocaust. Death has come in many guises, Genocide, starvation, civil war, disease and simply murder. Those campaigners, and I could name many of them, have the blood of millions of Africans on their hands, men women and children. Tragically, men women and children will continue to die, until the government of Africa is taken out of the hands of Negro people and into the hands of the ASG. It is interesting to note that although most of the apologists for African failure point to the absence of education being of the first importance; most of the evil dictators of Africa have received a high level of education from European University's.

The difference between a civilised man and an uncivilised man is the quality of compassion, Africa is bereft of compassion.

As oil runs out, Africa will cease to receive handouts from the Western world. African oil will be seized by European or Far Eastern powers and much of Africa will revert to savagery almost over night.

Africa destroys itself and then feeds on the wreckage. Africa does not deserve aid and aid is counterproductive. Africa needs complete change of government and if all current African governments could be removed it would be well for all Africans.

The horrific pictures we are constantly exposed to on television showing emaciated and decease ridden African children will not be cured by charity. To remove this blight on human society we must remove the African governments who create this problem. No government composed only of Negro people can possibly succeed.

CHAPTER SEVEN

THE CHINESE THREAT

Famously, Napoleon is reported to have remarked, "Let China sleep, the world will tremble when she wakes" Napoleon was right and China is awake and yes the world should tremble.

China is the most alien of all the evolutionary groups, containing and conditioned by a group mind that contains values not recognisable in Western civilisation. Because of the physical differences in the palaeontology of the Chinese it is possible that they have evolved from one of the 'radiant groups' which appeared two million years ago. This possibility may explain the fundamental differences in the evolved mind of the Chinese when valued against the West. China's isolation from the rest of mankind for most of those two millions of years has exaggerated the basic difference that naturally exists between China and Western Europe. China's huge population and ability to absorb technology is leading to a growth in economic power that is nothing short of explosive. This dynamic growth will mean that China will overtake the USA in economic power in about twenty- thirty years. That in itself gives rise to serious consequences for the West but more serious still is the almost certain probability that China will embark on a huge military expansion.

The probability of this expansion is underlined by Chinese weakness in the supply of oil. With current rates of economic growth, China in twenty years will be consuming half as many barrels a day as Saudi Arabia is producing at this time. In the 2030's as oil supply around the world becomes seriously competitive, China will have to move to protect its supplies. China will not hesitate to use its military muscle to ensure supply. Remember that China is a fully capable atomic power. Equally armed, Chinese forces will easily beat any other group for two reasons. 1) Numbers of men who can be put in the field, this number in some cases greater than the whole populations of other countries, and 2) The mind set of the Chinese which gladly accepts battlefield death and the willingness of their commanders to use that factor.

Internal problems as well as those arising from their increasing dependence on imported oil will push China into an aggressive foreign policy. This probability is hidden at the moment as China absorbs the culture and economic practice of the West. Because of the nature of the Chinese State the prosperity created by China's increasing industrial might, will not percolate down to the population on an even basis. There will be widespread problems with dispossessed peasants and general rural unemployment.

China will seek to avoid a direct confrontation with the USA in the early advancing years of this century but will be prepared to directly confront Japan and Russia in its search for secure oil. Taiwan will increasingly become an international bone of contention and China will use this bone to test American resolution.

The first aggressive action in the oil wars is likely to be the Chinese action to take control of any oil in the Sea of Japan. Japan will learn by then, that they will not be able to rely on American help when that time arrives.

Relationships between India and China in these early years of the century are key. India's economy is growing almost as fast as China and will contribute to the shortage of oil world-wide. India will never, however, present the same military threat as will China. Unfortunately however, India has an exaggerated view of its own military might and it is conceivable that a dispute over growing economic influence could arise between India and China and that such a dispute could trigger military action. In the circumstances where India got involved in a conflict with China, India would be overwhelmed easily.

The West's relationship with China will deteriorate on two fronts,:-

1) The growing ability of the Chinese to supply any product cheaper than the West will mean embargoes and trade controls. This will happen simply because of the economically catastrophic effect on Western economies of cheap Chinese imports.

2) China will begin to seek guaranteed markets in the remainder of the Eastern world and will become aggressive in securing these.

When natural supplies of oil run out in the later part of this century or as oil becomes a scarce commodity; China will be willing to embark aggressively on any action to secure its future. By that time, China will be more powerful militarily than any other two nations on earth. This is the moment of truth for all those who have peddled the concept of the universal nature of humanity. China will seek to serve China only, irrespective of the effect on the rest of the world.

The world will necessarily need to get used to the fact that after about 2020 any world decisions will depend on China's attitude

Conclusion

There can be no doubt that there are wide differences of human value expression and behaviour patterns, which clearly separate the primary human racial groups. These differences have no connection with intelligence and I do not seek to suggest a hierarchy of intellectual capability. The differences are a reflection of separate evolutionary experiences imprinting behavioural standards over very long periods of time.

Having looked at a number of the great races of mankind and mused on their different performances on the great stage of history, how, other than accepting our notion of the evolutionary mind can we explain the extraordinary differences that obviously exist between them? It is my position that only the reality of evolutionary forces at work on the human mind can account for such a wide divergence of ability and social performance. If we look at the two thousand years since Christ, the widely differing performance of the primary races can only be explained by evolutionary differences.

It is important to remember always that the other levels of evolutionary development among mankind are not our enemies, but then neither are they our friends; they are in fact our responsibility. In the land of the blind, he who has sight must ensure that the blind do not destroy themselves by failure to see danger.

Those who refuse to accept the truth of evolutionary consciousness must find explanations for the differences in racial behaviour, which so clearly exist. The choice for the ASG is clear, recognise the reality of differing evolutionary consciousness and continue human development as we have in these last centuries or deny the truth of these differences and face a decline into sub-standard human development and catastrophic social disaster. In the USA, in Britain, in Germany, and in all the other ASG States, people must recognise that it is more important to be ASG than to be American, German or British.

It is possible to ignore the clear and developing danger from cross-evolutionary meltdown and it is so easy to mouth platitudes which exude sweetness and light, brotherly love and all encompassing compassion without regard to consequences and it may make you feel good to go that route. This route however is the route to extinguishing the light of ASG civilisation and ushers in the horrors of a possible Second Dark Age

THE CONSEQUENCES

The inevitable consequences of cross evolutionary blending or breeding are very predictable, with many examples in history.

Some members of the population of an unsuccessful level of evolution will seek to transfer their life prospects to a successful evolutionary group. In so doing, and who can blame them for the attempt, they will bring with them the genetic makeup of their failed society or racial group. A successful evolutionary race, can of course absorb, a small percentage of incoming lower order evolutionary migrants without too many serious consequences. However when the incoming group of migrants reaches a significant percentage of the host population, then genetic trends are set up which in time lead to the complete alteration of the host nation's characteristics.

We have seen this in physical reality many times in history and I am always persuaded that the example of Imperial Rome is as good as any, when illustrating this mechanism. By whatever mechanism of locality and racial breeding a small tribe in central Italy became the dominant human group in the centuries immediately before A.D. Ancient Rome had a society that protected decision making within a small core of aristocratic families and consequently the identity of Rome was not quickly thrown open to a massive change by alien gene introduction.

Unfortunately, Rome like all great nations of the time, was a slave state and began the large scale importation of slaves from every area of the then known world. These slaves would bring with them the genes of perhaps four of the evolutionary groups identified in this book. It has been said, that in the early imperial period, for every single freeborn Roman there were 1000 slaves held in bondage. Inevitably as the result of sexual attraction, many cross evolutionary children would inevitably be created and in the fullness of time the whole nature of Rome changed and those who we knew as the

Roman became the people we know as the Latins, in Italy France and Spain.

The USA is now absorbing huge numbers of lower level evolutionary peoples and the effect is inevitable. The ASG nature and behaviour of the USA will change and will more likely resemble the failed societies of South America. Until the late twenties and early thirty's of the twentieth century the core immigration group into the US states was from ASG countries. In the twenties and thirties there was large scale Latin immigration into the North Eastern States of the USA. With the arrival of the Italian into most of the large cities of this region, the nature of those cities subtly changed.

The USA occupies a position in the world, similar to that held by ancient Rome in its possession of political power, and the fall of the USA which has already begun, will have just as serious an effect as did the fall of Rome.

Turning to more parochial expressions of cross evolutionary breeding, citizens in ASG societies have to come to terms with some uncomfortable facts. That lovely black man who is your neighbour, who keeps his property up to standard and is a good friend when needed, carries in his gene bank the death of the society that enables you to enjoy his company and enables him to behave in the way he does. Should his gene bank become the standard of your society then the familiar practices of our high level civilisation will deteriorate and eventually be extinguished under a new level of evolutionary people. Evolutionary standards can not be considered with individuals. Racial behaviour is illustrated by group behaviour in the country or society of origin.

Do not, under any circumstances, try to judge a racial group by the behaviour of a single individual known to you from that racial group. A lower evolutionary racial group member will take on all the superficial appearance and behaviour of the host group as long as he remains a minority. When that condition changes, the incomer will revert to his racial group's standards and morality. The pleasant hotel staff who serves you in your holiday hotel in Tunisia and attracts your admiration, is a member of a racial group with the highest number of recruits to ISIS from North Africa. Leopards can not change their spots and racial groups can not perform outside their evolutionary experiences.

There is a simple choice for the existing ASG societies. The first choice is to do nothing and continue to mouth platitudes of human equality and value and as a consequence watch, as our civilisation declines into something less than it currently is. The second choice is much harder to achieve, signal an acceptance of the philosophy of this small book and take all the measures necessary to preserve the identity of the ASG.

If you accept the philosophy of this small book, you will no longer be puzzled by the animal behaviour of some societies in the Middle East and in Africa. It is our, (The ASG) responsibility to chastise these aberrant nations and keep them in a controlled evolutionary setting for as long as it takes to permanently influence their behaviour. That is the only action which will guarantee the onward progression of the Human Race.

There are those who will argue that within our own ASG societies, there exist low intelligence and morally decrepit people who do not practice our standards. This is true, but the way the gene bank works means that even the idiot child of an ASG racial member carries within them the successful gene standards that are the result of thousands of evolutionary years.

The effect of the assimilation of a significant 'other level' evolutionary population is a subtle mechanism, at first members of the other evolutionary group are recognisable easily, but as the process continues the distinction between the host and the incomer is blurred and becomes difficult to identify. The incomers, whilst difficult to now identify, are still carrying their unsuccessful gene bank and diluting the host gene bank.

CHAPTER EIGHT.

THE FALL OF THE USA

The decline of the USA carries with it enormous dangers for the entire world for as that decline accelerates socially and diplomatically, the USA will still be an enormous military power. The USA has since inception been guided in its policies by ASG politicians and the world could always rely on responses by the USA which were in the interest of all peoples. Now that the control of the destiny of the USA slips ever further into the hands of Afro Caribbean or Latin peoples, we will no longer be able to rely on the responses of this dying power being in the interest of mankind in general. The decay of Military power may take up to half a century longer than social decay. This will be a period of extreme danger for the world.

Despite the oft-repeated cliché that the USA is a melting pot, the reality is that the country has historically been dominated and run by the ASG. Apart from the forcible migration of black slaves who until recently were not part of the assimilation process, the migratory group into the USA up until the mid 1850s was mostly composed from ASG roots, British, German, Dutch and Scandinavian. The population established by this movement was large enough to carry its control momentum up to the present day. That control began to change in the early part of the twentieth century with the arrival of large numbers of Italian and Spanish immigrants. The nature of the great cities of Western USA changed fundamentally with this new intake and the process of decay had set in. This decay was hastened by the migration of Afro-

Caribbean people from the southern States of the USA into the industrial North East of the USA. The domination of the USA by the ASG is now finally slipping away and the USA will probably split into a number of countries before the end of the current century.

One of the problems for the USA and as a result a problem for the rest of the world, is that the USA is the first Super Power in history to arrive at that pinnacle of power simply because of its size and manufacturing strength. All of the previous holders of the position of supreme world power have achieved that position by centuries of struggle, both social and military. The ability to manage that power is inherent in the successful management of those struggles. In the USA no such struggles have taken place. The USA grew to size and strength behind the benevolent and total British command of the seas and oceans of the world. When Britain controlled the world's oceans, no hostile expedition could be planned without British permission. The USA was left in isolation to take whatever land they wished in North America. The society that they engaged to manage their affairs was simply transplanted from the experience of Europe, again largely from the British. In all these matters there was no experience of the management of growth in society, in military terms the USA had to deal with a few Neolithic savages in the form of Red Indians. Very able propaganda has however elevated these struggles with a prehistoric people to ludicrous importance. Thus a savage chief, Geronimo, who never had more than a handful of men, is better known across the world than the men who saved civilisation in the Peninsular War. The so-called Battle of Little Big-Horn would be considered as a minor skirmish with hostile's by Britain in its days of Empire, yet this skirmish is better known by the young of the West than the heroic crossing of the Douro or the storming of Ciudad Roderigo. Hostile armies never threatened the cities of the USA, and the illusion of military might other than 'hardware might' was created. This social illusion created by Hollywood and fostered by all politicians' forms the base of an enormous danger to the USA.

In this critical period of US decline, the growth of Chinese manufacturing power is yet another dimension whose influence is only dimly understood by the West. Chinese manufacturing power with its consequential transfer of purchasing power from the USA and Europe to Asia was at the root of the 2008 sub prime collapse. Western entrepreneurs have eagerly used cheap labour markets to achieve higher profits but have not of course been aware of the consequences of the transfer of manufacturing power brought about by their actions. The effect on the economy of the USA is potentially catastrophic.

I have travelled widely and often in the USA since the 70's and have loved the ASG area of that country. Moving away from the burgeoning and alien cities of the Northeast and into the real heart of the old USA is a pleasant travel experience. Places like Vermont, upstate Pennsylvania, Kentucky, Ohio, Iowa and Wisconsin show life in the near ideal condition. Unfortunately the USA which has been so attractive and which I have enjoyed, like so many others, is in decline and on the current course is doomed.

In the Southwest of the USA the burgeoning Latin population will eventually dominate this area of the country and new and non-ASG aspirations will emerge. In this area already, you are unlikely to meet English speaking service help in most of the Hotels. In the Northeast of the USA the inbound numbers of non-ASG immigrants has become an overwhelming flood and the nature of the USA will slowly be affected by this input.

Most significantly, we today observe the United States of America engaged in the active process of assimilating a population of some thirty five million Negro's into the main body of the administrating group of ASG. The thirty five million figure is the number provided by the USA 2001 census figures, this number is less than the perception one receives traveling in the USA and is probably the result of incorrect labeling, which reduces the real figure. As a result of this assimilation and markedly as this century goes on, the American decision making process will falter and social organisation will begin to erode (it is already eroding) and eventually the decline of the United States will be complete. This process may take most of this century and may end with the USA breaking into a number of countries. The destruction of the USA is being mirrored by most of the European members of the ASG. The simple process of racial assimilation is accomplishing the destruction of the USA where powerful military opponents could only fail.

The decline of the USA is already evident to anyone travelling across that continent. I myself have travelled extensively in the 'States and recently I was able to observe many examples of the evolutionary decline already evident. Anyone who wishes to observe the American of tomorrow has only to have a close look at the periphery of the capital city Washington. In these dreadful suburbs there is emerging a class of citizen who has no knowledge or interest in the traditions of the Great Democracy. They begin to be represented at all electoral levels and over the coming years they will collect a significant political power base. Their effect on the image of the society of the USA will be catastrophic. I myself have seen tomorrow's American administrator, he lives in these awful suburbs and he is not attractive and he is not ASG.

In many of the Southern States of the Union, well meaning affirmative programmes identified to ensure more black representation and employment, mean that many persons who would otherwise not achieve public representative status are now pushed forward. Increasingly, this means growing incompetence and falling standards of public service morality. If you wish to see a completed example of this trend, travel to the city of Cairo, made famous by the visit of Charles Dickens in the nineteenth century. The ASG have left Cairo and the town no longer looks or feels like the USA. On the Southwestern seaboard, the huge influx of Spanish immigrants is achieving similar effects. This influx of Hispanics is changing the nature of Southwestern USA society from an A.S.G. to South American Spanish.

For a foretaste of the effects of unlimited Spanish American immigration into the 'States, I recommend that whilst travelling in California, it is informative to leave the American city of San Diego and cross the border into Mexico's Bahia California. Crossing the border you cross the evolutionary line between a level one and two evolutionary group, you step from high quality, civilised development, into a human sewer of tragic proportions. If those who currently manage our affairs have their way this human sewer will extend to the Canadian border.

The worldwide media frenzy over the election of Barrack Obama is a sad reflection on the institutional blindness of political commentators. His story is a modern version of the King with no clothes fable. This is of course the regular standard that has been experienced throughout history. The enthusiastic fools crowing over the election of Obama for all the wrong reasons are the same people who stood and cheered when Nero took the crown of imperial Rome or those who enthusiastically welcomed Robert Mugabe as the savior of Africa when he took the keys of Rhodesia from Ian Smith. Not that I am suggesting that Obama will behave as those particular madmen behaved. Obama has said nothing that will change the world. He has identified no particular policy future that will make a difference, so we will be left to discover whether he is even an average competent administrator. Obama comes to power not as a harbinger of the beginning of a new golden age for the USA but as an indicator that we have arrived at the beginning of the end of the American dream.

Obama was elected simply because he is black and his election is an illustration of the destructive triumph of two separate groups in the USA. The first group is the emerging Afro/American voter, the second group are the overcivilised middleclass voters who have been raised on a diet of liberal nonsense all of their lives.

NB This note added on the 7th November 2012.

An interesting phenomenon of the re-election of Obama as President is an examination of the geographical areas in which he reached his success. The majority of the States

declaring for Obama are either Latin dominated states or States having significant populations drawn from recent immigration. In a later chapter I forecast the breakup of the USA into three separate countries toward the end of the 21st century. The voting patterns of the November 2012 election prejudge that breakup with their localized identity. This demographic election phenomenon will mean the likely end of alternating periods of Democratic party and Republican party governments.

In the modern period, travel means are accessible easily and the migration of socio-economic groups seeking life improvements has been accelerated immensely. This form of migration will and is changing the world we know very rapidly and will effectively destroy the power of the West.

Because of the reality that socio-economic migration is driven by the ***failure*** of the parent culture to provide, it is a melancholy fact that the incoming migrants are more likely to bring genetic traits which will transfer that inability to provide or habit of failure into the host country. The simple fact is that their group genes in their old habitat failed to provide the decent life and in this new and alien environment it is likely that their group performance will remain the same and influence a successful environment into failure. This means that efficiency in administration and distribution will decline to reflect the incoming gene level of failed performance. This is a slow process and imperceptibly and irretrievably acceptable standards of achievement will decline. The USA has already begun the assimilation of the thirty-five million migrants of African stock forcibly transferred as slaves. This single genetic ingredient alone will completely alter the nature of the USA in the fullness of time as the assimilation moves toward completion.

When and if the existing process of multi-race assimilation in the USA is completed, you will have achieved the 'coffee coloured people' so beloved by song writers but you will not have achieved a caring, providing, successful society heading for the stars. You will have produced a South American type continent set in inevitable decline and unable to deal with the giant problems that faces the human race.

This process of assimilation under discussion has already occurred and the results are available for study. The entire continent of South America is the place where the consequences of cross-evolutionary breeding have been most fully experienced. The results are tragic. In a continent that has as a natural right the benefits of almost all of nature's gifts of terrain and resource, yet the people live in poverty and despair. Those human rights which we in the ASG expect as a birthright are largely absent, and the benefits of mans journey through history are not available to the majority of South Americans. If we sit and do nothing in this first decade of the twenty-first century then the whole of North America will become a huge extension of the South American Type society. This consequence is a simple choice that the people of today who are still in possession of their ASG birthright have to make. The problem is to convince people that the results arising from that process are inevitable. The society and people produced by this process will resemble the South American Latin and their proven record in the administration of land and people is covered in some depth in the chapter headed "How did they perform?" I would expect this new group of people to perform at the sort of level described in that chapter.

The willingness of the ASG to enthusiastically embrace the dilution of their own people and standards is itself a product of over-civilisation and advanced humanitarianism which does not exist at any other human evolutionary level. This condition of over-civilisation and advanced humanitarianism is itself a consequence of fully emancipated populations allowing poorly informed academics and malicious media full uncontrolled expression.

An additional danger for the USA is that unlike the UK, the USA has failed to limit the growth of internal military political leverage and because the judiciary in the States is not independent of the Government, this fact projects a further dimension to the crisis. There is a serious danger that under the pressures of financial collapse or demographic identities emerging, the USA will move toward a repressive military dictatorship "in the interests of public safety". If this occurred it would hasten the break-up of the USA.

The decline of the USA is not simply a matter of race because that problem this time round comes at the same time as a world financial problem begins to develop which will exacerbate the social problems already discussed. From about 2010 onward the era of cheap energy will come to an end. Oil will become an increasingly scarce commodity and the increasing cost of that scarce commodity will of itself drive all of the industrial nations into heavy recession. The USA, which at this time is the greatest per capita user of energy, will feel the growing shortage of oil more severely than any other nation. The Great Recession of the 1930's will appear as Comfort City compared with what will happen in the 40's of this 21st century. Later on, oil becomes a commodity that is scarce to the point where nations will fight to secure their own supply. The USA will have to decide whether to fight aggressively to secure its supplies of the black gold or to face the problem that it will need to reduce its population by a half.

If the USA wishes to ensure that its people in this century escape the worst effects of the oil crash then its governments will have to take actions unthinkable at this time. For instance the government of the USA in the thirties/forties of this century may have to seize the oil reserves of Mexico and deny Mexicans access to that oil. They may also have to take the same action in respect of Venezuelan oil.

Unlike all other previous human crisis, this one doesn't go away; it gets worse as the century ages. Looming behind these inevitable events, the growth in Chinese power threatens everything we have.

The first obvious signs of the crisis will become apparent in the twenties of this century when fuel costs will force drastic changes on the economic life of the US

Note added in December 2016. The election of Donald Trump is an illustration of the danger that the world faces in the decline of the USA, increasingly this kind of maverick politician will be in power in the USA with all the awful possible consequences inherent in that condition.

CHAPTER NINE.

THE END OF THE AGE OF OIL

As this 21st century ages, the growing scarcity of oil will create economic conditions that will make the year of 2008 seem like comfort city. People who live through the end of the age of oil will face conditions of collapse perhaps only previously experienced by those who lived through the fall of the Roman Empire. All of the pillars which make up the accepted face of Western civilisation will come crashing down and for perhaps a further century the human race will be preoccupied with survival rather than as now with pleasure and comfort.

The leadership of the world's great stock markets, which have contributed to the enormous growth of personal prosperity, will come to an end with an almighty crash. As the cost of oil soared through the $100 per barrel level the world experienced the 2008 crash. As oil reaches $200+ a barrel, a total meltdown of the financial world as we know it will take place and in the vacuum created by this crash the social divisions which exist in the USA will tear that country apart. Oil then becomes a scarce commodity and many nations will be denied any access to oil. They will fight or starve or more probably both. No international aid will be possible and Africa will revert to savagery within a few short years. The world as we know it will be at an end and the new Dark Age will be upon us.

In the early decades of this century, oil will fluctuate in price and availability commensurate with the level of economic activity the world is engaged in at that time. This does not alter the forward projection of ultimate scarcity and complete exhaustion.

As the century goes on, fuel for general transportation, civil aircraft, motorcars and ships will be strictly rationed and the era of international leisure travel and the investment that activity generates will disappear. By the middle 40's of this century some countries will have no access at all to oil and will face starvation and war. The USA will have residual oil deposits but will guard them jealously and strictly ration their use. There will be a need to reduce the acreage of food crops and increase the acreage of synthetic fuel crops. This of course will compound the cycle of food shortages and bring about starvation in countries that rely on foodstuffs from the USA and Canada.) Major countries like China have real difficulties in obtaining oil and will prepare aggressive actions to ensure supply. International travel for ordinary citizens is a dream of the past. The tourist nations, Spain Italy Turkey etc. will have experienced dramatic shrinkage of economy and are effectively beggar nations.

Oil is a finite resource and the consumption of that resource is measurable and predictable. Oil ***will*** run out, probably toward the end of this century. However, just as importantly, long before it runs out, oil will have become a scarce commodity and the entire world will be plunged into a hideous maelstrom of decline. Whilst Global Warming is a real threat over the medium term, the immediate threat to civilisation is the end of the age of oil

The effect of the end of supplies of oil will mean the deaths of millions by military conflict and probably a billion people as a consequence of starvation brought about by the failure of oil.

Oil is the end product of the decay of vegetable matter over millions of years. Mighty jungles and forests where no man heard a tree fall and which contributed in life to the atmosphere we now breathe are the source of our black gold. Buried in the mantle of the earth the decay of these ancient forests over millions of years has given us the short-lived miracle of oil.

Why will the end of oil lead to military conflict?

1) Because if you are the ruler or the people of a country that has no natural oil resource and the world market denies you supply or you simply cannot afford the world market price. You as a country will have the simple choice of fight for oil or die.

2) Countries like China with small reserves of oil and who are dependent on the supply from around the world are among the few nations who will have the military capability to take their oil from whomever they target.

3) The first signs of real scarcity of oil will become a recognisable reality sometime in the late twenties of this century and by that time China will be a true superpower whose will can only be obstructed by destructive military means. To the Chinese mentality it would be foolish to refrain from the use of your most potent weapons in a war of survival. China has always been prepared to sacrifice millions of her own people in her struggles and will do so again.

Why will the end of oil lead to starvation?

1) Because the production of most foods is underpinned by the use of oil or its derivatives. Listening to alternative fuel lobbies is like trying to swim with metal boots. It is impossible to continue food production at even its current rate without plentiful supplies of oil. Bear in mind that a significant portion of the globe is already undernourished, couple that with the view that the world population will double by 2025 and the recipe for massive suffering is already in place.

2) Because many pesticides essential to agriculture are made or derived from oil products, additionally, nearly all fertilisers are made from oil derivatives.

3) An additional phenomenon is that food-producing areas by the million acre will have to be turned over to the growth of plants for the production of lubricants and bio-fuels. Food will become as scarce as oil and our children and our grandchildren will experience the nightmare of a world where millions are starving to death.

When will the oil run out?

FACT. Oil supply is already declining and by the middle thirties will begin to become truly scarce, the price of world oil will escalate and the first effects of the economic reality brought about by that fact will be begin to be felt. At first this effect will be the traditional one of stock market collapse and mass unemployment; this will be followed almost immediately by nations competing for supply. As the century wears on this conflict will become highly volatile and massive conflicts will erupt. Traditional western views on the universality of human rights, if not cast to the winds will bring the destruction of the West.

What are the facts

Dick Chaney said in a speech in 1999 that there would be a 2% growth in annual oil demand and a 3% decline in production of available oil. Both these numbers now seem to be massively understated. The view of the oil wise community is now that oil demand will rise by 5% and that the decline in oil production may well proceed at between 6-10%. None of these figures include the raising of Africa to a satisfactory standard of living. If investment and industrialisation took off anywhere in Africa, these estimates of use and decline would need to be pushed higher.

The discovery of new reserves of oil peaked in 1962 and has declined ever since. Of course some new reserves will be discovered, but insufficient to make a difference to the awful scenario being unfolded in this book. The extraction of shale oil is attracting a high level of interest at the moment and will provide a small stimulus to oil supply over twenty years.

Currently we are consuming about 30 billion barrels a year and as the industrialisation of China and India and indeed all of the Far East progresses, this figure will continue to rise. That is, it would continue to rise, if supplies were available; supplies are already inadequate to provide for even a small part of this growth.

What makes the coming disaster the more frightening is the realisation that all of the figures necessary to make these predictions have been available to our political leaders for many years. Almost nothing has been done to avert the crisis, indeed policies have been pursued which are likely to exacerbate the problem. Mealy-mouthed politicians mumble about alternative and renewable energy, when the pursuit of such things is fairy tale land, pure unadulterated fantasy. Understand that the politicians making these comments are aware of the fantasy of alternative energy.

Of course there will be a role for alternative and renewable energy but at its best, this role will only supply a minute portion of the energy currently being consumed on a daily basis.

The effect of the end of the oil age comes in two parts; first, oil becomes a scarce and expensive commodity. Sometime in the late twenties there will be no surplus oil and costs will rise astronomically. This will lead to the collapse of the world economic order, as we know it. Secondly as the century ends, there will be a total absence of oil and the new Dark Age will have truly begun. By the time the oil actually runs out, the population of the world will have declined significantly, mostly as a result of starvation, and such things as everyday global travel for ordinary people will be a thing of history.

The people who live in the middle years of this century will go through the same sort of experiences that the people of Europe went through at the time of the fall of the Roman Empire in the fourth century. The established order will collapse and only the strongest will survive.

Electricity supply will become wholly dependent on nuclear generation and that leads to yet another but more distant problem, in that uranium is itself a relatively scarce commodity. Fortunately fast breeder technology will give us very long-term protection from any shortages of this fuel. In any case Uranium, unlike oil, is a substance that will exist elsewhere in the solar system and the need to obtain that resource when it arises will eventually generate the provision needed for real space programmes.

Air transport will feel the full effects of the rising price of oil in the late twenties of this century. Costs of flying will soar and the era of cheap overseas travel will come to an abrupt end. Aeroplane construction will dive and companies like Boeing and European Airbus will shed many thousands of jobs and by themselves affect the economy of a number of nations. Countries whose major overseas earnings come from cheap travel and tourism like Spain and Portugal will find themselves with empty towns and deserted Urbanisation's as the ex-pats go home.

Most Cross-Atlantic travel will be by nuclear powered ships or giant and super efficient sailing or steam ships. Luxury travel across the Atlantic will be by nuclear powered liners. In enlightened countries most electricity generation will be by nuclear plants and all dwellings, by law, will be fitted with solar power capability.

The new age of steam will mean that in some countries rail travel will be by new super efficient engines as we begin again the re-exploitation of coal and wood. The electrification of all rail transport is essential where the nation concerned has nuclear power.

The human tragedy of the end of the Age of Oil is the more poignant in that this end is and was entirely forcastable. Many government officials have gone to their graves guiltily knowing that the problem, too huge for them to deal with, would come back to haunt their descendants.

Had humanity earlier grasped the reality of race and the frailty of fossil fuel supply, the coming disaster could have been prevented and humanity might now have been looking forward to another millennium of triumph. Instead the 21st century will be the graveyard of many of humanities dreams and an experience of social horror not known since the fall of Rome. Much could still be done to mitigate the fall, but if this is to be the case the action needs to start now.

NOTE ADDED 2015

a) The current downturn in the price of oil is a temporary phenomenon only, and does not prejudice the forecasts' of the end of oil. These price dips will occur cyclically as world manufacture grows and contracts.

b) Fracking and shale oil extraction will extend the age of oil but for a comparatively short period.

CHAPTER TEN

THE MUSLIM THREAT.

The religion founded by the Prophet Mohammed is fundamentally irreconcilable with the nature of Western civilisation. The religion of Jesus Christ is a gentle epistle of humanity. The Muslim faith is the only major world religion, which directly advocates violence and slavery within its founder's treatise 'The Koran'.

Many politicians when discussing the current role of the Muslim faith in world-wide terrorism are anxious, whilst such discussions are being held, to foster and support the belief that terrorism is contrary to the teachings of the Koran. This belief is simply not true. The Koran expressly authorises violence in the conversion of 'infidels' to the Muslim faith. It is probable that the politicians mouthing these platitudes have never read the Koran. It is even more likely that the politicians are pursuing their ever-consuming political correctness. The Koran makes quite clear that the killing of infidels (Us) is holy business and it is particularly identified as a duty. Some of those instructions as an example are listed here.

It is clear in the Koran that Muslim teaching separates all mankind into "believers and infidels" and advocates very different treatment for Muslims as against all of the rest of us grouped as infidels. Treatment of Muslims in the Koran equates very closely to treatment advocated by most of the other great religions (except in the case of women). Treatment of the infidel however is very different, with numerous exhortations to engage in great slaughter and enslavement. Here is a short list of the many such exhortations to violence drawn directly from the Koran.

1) No prophet hath been enabled to take captives until he had made great slaughter in the earth (Sura 8).

2) And when the sacred months are passed, kill those who join other gods with God wherever ye shall find them, and seize them, besiege them, and lay wait for them with every kind of ambush. (Sura 9).

3) Verily, of the faithful hath God bought their persons and their substance, on condition of Paradise and for them in return: on the path of God shall they fight, and slay, and be slain, a promise for this is pledged in the Law and in the Koran. (Sura 9. This is the Sura generally used to legitimise terrorists.)

4) Believers! Wage war against such of the infidels, as are your neighbours, and let them know you are rigorous. (Sura 9).

5) When ye encounter the infidels, strike off their heads till ye have made great slaughter amongst them, and of the rest make fast the fetters, (Sura 47).

6) They desire that ye should be infidels, as they are infidels, and that ye should be alike. Take therefore none of them for friends, till they have fled their homes for the cause of God. If they turn back, then seize them, and slay them wherever ye find them; but take non of them for friends.(Sura 4)

These comments are not merely observations; the Muslim faithful believe that these are instructions from the word of God.

The Koran avers that women are inferior to men and are the chattels of men. Whilst piously condemning fornication, the Koran goes on to authorise the use of women slaves for sex and exploitation. This duel standard runs through all of the teaching of the Muslim faith. Within Mohammed's own lifetime, the teachings of Islam had resulted in the deaths of thousands of 'infidels'.

The Koran on women.

1) Men are superior to women on account of the qualities with which God hath gifted the one above the other, and on account of their substance for them.(Sura4)

2) Forbidden to you also are married women, except those who are in your hands as slaves. (Its Ok to fornicate with slaves, married or otherwise).(Sura 4).

The Koran on friendship and neighbourliness.

1) O believers! Take not the Jews or Christians as friends. They are but one another's friends. If any one of you taketh them for his friends, he surely is one of them. (Sura 5)

The primary objective of the Islamic faith is the conversion of all peoples to that faith and to legitimise the use of violence to achieve that end. This is not a subsidiary objective; it is the prime objective of this dangerous faith.

In its identification of the supremacy of the Koran teachings as against any concept of personal rights or intellectual discussion of reality the Muslim religion stifles human progression. Any Christian would repudiate the kinds of instructions contained in the examples above if such abnormalities were contained in the Christian Bible.

Any Christian can discuss any tenet of the Bible and express his/her own opinion on that tenet. Such discussion on the Koran is not possible for Muslims because they are obliged to regard every item of expression within the Koran as the definitive word of god. No matter how trivial or meaningless or criminal in the light of modern knowledge some of those elements might be, all of the contents of the Koran must be digested whole. Such a position is intellectual slavery and has an enormous effect on Muslim society.

To suggest that the Christian West can live alongside the Muslim faith is the same as suggesting that democracy can live alongside Nazism. It is simply not possible for this coexistence to continue.

It may be necessary to declare that the practice of the Muslim faith is incompatible with the standards of life, which we require in Western Christian society.

All who live in the shadow of the minaret have no peace, there is no humanity, there is only the promise of death. There is only misery and despair. The Muslim religion is the antithesis of Christianity; it is a negation of all human values.

CHAPTER ELEVEN.

A COMMENTARY ON THE ELEMENTS OF SOCIAL DESTRUCTION AT WORK IN THE WORLD TODAY.

All those who seek to settle in the UK or indeed in any of the great Western democracies as economic migrants, do so simply because the society they flee from has failed to provide the kind of environment that we enjoy as a right. The societies that they flee from have in many circumstances infinitely more resource than does the UK but what they don't have of course, is an ASG leadership to organise their country.

Immigration of the levels that the UK has experienced over three decades now means that the attractive society which these immigrants seek and perceive in our country is threatened by the assimilation of these different evolutionary minds into our social fabric. The long term assimilation of these people will remove the attractive society our ancestors built and replace it with a dysfunctional society of the kind they have left.

Why do the societies they flee from fail? Simply because they are who they are. Libya is a classic example of the result of over civilised thinking confusing the reality of a disorderly people and believing that simply giving these people a free choice will result in a better society. The society they have created since Khadafy is worse than the tyranny he represented.

When you watch the endless pictures of emaciated African babies dying from malnourishment, whose fault is this tragedy? In most cases the national governments of these unfortunates are the recipients of huge sums of regular national aid which is spent on a variety of projects, most of which are simply a waste of money. The truth is of course that these governments are incapable of social organisation; they are still hunter gathers and nothing more.

The world is racked by war and terrorism; these are the effects of the taboo subject of race not having been discussed at all over the last 70 years. The idiotic vision of serious politicians from ASG countries talking to representatives of these awful societies and attempting by exhortation to create new ways forward would be funny if it were not tragic. We have turned the world over to the ugliest societies that have been produced by mankind so far. We who had the power at the start of the twentieth century to guarantee that mankind moved forward toward universal quality of life surrendered the right by listening to the corrosive drivel that over civilised societies always produce.

The recent demonstration of contempt for the rule of law which was expressed in a major sporting institution was very illustrative in racial terms. Although it was clear that Sepp Blatter had presided over an infinitely corrupt organisation, nevertheless he was overwhelmingly re-elected to lead that organisation. The whole number of the African countries voted for Blatter, not surprising, because to them (the African Countries) corruption is endemic and they know no other way of doing business. They would have been surprised if the organiser's fingers were not in the till. If we were unfortunate enough to have a world government at this time it would be dominated by these awful people and simply be massively corrupt just like FIFA. Interestingly two Latin countries also voted for Blatter

For the past two hundred years the world has been led by two ASG nations, from 1815 until 1918 by the British and thereafter by the USA. The USA is in rapid decline and there is no other ASG nation to take up the burden. Australia will require another seventy years before she reaches majority. The decline of the USA is extremely dangerous for mankind in general terms. Despite the rapid growth of a dysfunctional society the USA will remain militarily very strong for most of this century. This strength in the hands of incompetents could bring untold risks.

We who were the victors in 1945 over the forces of darkness thought we had left a proper vehicle for the management of human affairs in our construction of the great tower by the river in New York to house the United Nations.

N.B. The following paragraphs were written in 2015 and have of course been overtaken by history in some areas, never the less the premises described are accurate and true

THE UNITED NATIONS

The UN building beside the river in New York was built as a tower of hope by the English speaking peoples and their allies at the end of the Second World War when we had defeated the forces of darkness.

It was supposed to be a place where despotism and tyranny would be confronted, where the weak would be defended and where, we the strong, would ensure that all governments pursued the standards of life which we expect as a right, for all of the people of the Earth.

These aspirations have been ignored and the UN has accomplished nothing. Many, certainly a majority, of those nations which sit in the chamber of the UN are themselves the representatives of tyranny and despotism. A majority of the members practice human rights abuses and a majority of the members have no concept of personal freedom.

The inhuman phenomenon of ISIS is a classic situation which should be confronted by the UN. ISIS needs, not to be militarily confronted, but needs to be exterminated. The UN could theoretically put one million men onto the ground in

Iraq and mop up all ISIS manpower in weeks. It will not do so because its voting power is in the hands of people who have little interest in justice.

The UN is useless and an unnecessary expense for the UK. What the world needs is a United ASG assembly with the power and the guts to use that power in the interests of the people of this world. The first article of this new assembly would be; No government is acceptable unless it fulfils the criteria of civilisation which we demand as a right.

The massive migration of Middle East people fleeing the war torn areas of Syria, Iraq and many North African nations must not be allowed to continue, if it does, the whole nature of Europe will be changed. The problem will only be solved when we make the countries these people are fleeing from fit to live in. That can only be achieved by aggressive removal of the unfit governments who have charge of these countries.

If the United Nations were to become meaningful, it would mean that a significant number of the member nations would need to be expelled from the organisation as being practitioners of antidemocratic social organisations and offending against any meaningful human rights. This of course won't happen; instead these governments will be invited to take part in decision making policy within the UN.

If an international organisation based on ASG member countries only were to be erected and given power to act on behalf of the worlds dispossessed then there might be a chance of real operational success.

European Union

The membership of the European Union has cost Britain up to 1,000,000 jobs since we joined this ill-fated ship. The balance of trade has shifted inexorably in favor of Europe each year of our membership. This fact is a matter of record. The idiotic presentation by Edward Heath suggested that British industry would take an ever larger share of Europe's market in the coming years after joining, but the reality is that Europe has taken an ever larger share of the British market since day one.

It is not only the loss of the jobs that is significant but the loss of many industries which are essential to the security and prosperity of our Nation have also been lost. Our Machine tool industry, absolutely essential to our defense requirements, has been almost totally lost together with the special skills and practices which this industry demanded. The loss of the Fishing industry has been fatal for many communities in the North of England and, because of indiscipline by European fisheries, even more fatal to our fish stocks .The total elimination of our steel industry carries enormous consequences for our national security.

I hear grown men who are full time politicians talking about the loss of jobs which will result from our leaving the EU. If you ask them why would we lose those jobs? they reply that Britain will lose access to the German and French markets. You shake your head for their dim intelligence and gently suggest to them that Germany could not afford to lose its biggest single market for its cars and would stand on its head to ensure reciprocal trading. Whilst France would love to see British manufacturers excluded from the EU, France depends on British imports of many manufacturing and agricultural products to stay solvent. No way can France afford to lose that market and similarly would be forced into reciprocal trading arrangements.

Just as important as the loss of jobs and industries is the effect that the EU has on our National Identity. There is no society in Europe other than Great Britain which has a pedigree older than seventy years. Without exception they owe their existence to the heroism of the Anglo American war effort. The Battle of Britain just celebrated as an anniversary was a battle that saved the world not just Britain. All of the European countries owe their very existence to our success in that battle. Had Britain had been defeated in 1940/41 it is probable that the USA would not have entered the war. Many people are not aware that the USA never declared war on Germany and if Hitler in his madness had not declared war on the USA following Pearl Harbor, the USA might well have stayed only in the Pacific War

In this book I talk about the existence of a condition of over civilisation and over the past two hundred years, this condition has cost Britain dearly. Great Britain has been responsible for the destruction of three attempts to enslave Europe. Firstly the destruction of Napoleon, and then successively in the two World Wars. In our victories in all three of these conflicts, our over-civilised people failed to ensure the maximum return for Britain arising out of these victories. At the end of the Napoleonic war Britain was in possession of most of the French overseas territories. Incredibly we gave them back to France as a gesture of international goodwill. Similarly after the two world wars when our small exhausted nation had achieved the impossible and brought down two aspirant world conquerors, Britain did not ensure that as a nation, we received our reward. Churchill was a great war time leader but his behaviour at Yalta was a disgrace and ensured that the USA and Russia carved up the spoils.

Membership of the EU as a trading entity was a wonderful idea. Membership of the EU as a super state is a disaster for Great Britain and is a continuation of the nation destroying forces identified earlier in this book.

Great Britain has been the most successful nation in history so far, giving the world a common language and being responsible for the creation of the most desirable places to live on Earth. Great Britain was also the template for Parliamentary government. All of this success was generated by our splendid geographical isolation guaranteed by the existence of the Channel. Free to develop our own social mores and free to develop our own educational objectives and free to develop institutional freedom. These freedoms are now prejudiced by our giving powers over our society to nations that have only sketchy association with the kind of society we demand as a right.

All of the members who sit on the benches of the European Parliament do so as a consequence of half a million men from

Britain, the USA and Canada landing on the beaches on D Day. We have nothing to learn from the EU, they have much to learn from us.

Note added December 2016. This treatise on the European Common Market was written in 2014.

CHAPTER TWELVE.

THE EVIL PRESS

And the over civilised

In the UK we are under the management of the most evil press and media in the Western world. Fundamentally disloyal, deliberately orchestrating anti British causes, the controllers of this media will have to be dealt with great severity. The problem of the British press is the fact that within its ranks and all but invisible to ordinary scrutiny, people who have been raised as children to see England as an oppressor are in senior positions and pedalling their poison.

Many children from foreign backgrounds have as a daily diet from an early age the continual drip of anti-English sentiment. Many of those who fit into this category are extremely difficult to identify in that they merge into a normal background so effectively. This pollutant extends into their adult life and they feel no loyalty to England under any circumstances. As the editors or producers of influential programmes or articles they seek always to undermine British self-respect. The BBC is particularly involved in this programme of denial. This denial of truth manifests itself in many ways, from denial of the reality of history or to the most trivial detail. For instance, if you are watching a news cast and the BBC presenter describes a crime and adds that a man was seen running away, you should know immediately that the man seen running away was black. Had he been white the BBC would have said a white man was seen to run away from the scene. Similarly if the BBC visit a school and a tiny minority of the pupils are black, the cameras will concentrate exclusively on this minority. The purpose here is to accentuate the 'Multi Cultural' society myth, which in the main is not real or accepted by the majority of people in this country. This particular denial of truth is an insignificant detail in the overall picture but illustrates the BBC in their role of deciding for you what you should believe. The BBC is enthusiastic in attacking any form of minute failure with the British military and will not publish good news about British troops.

I have identified fifty BBC executives whom I believe are engaged in an active policy of denigration of anything British. These people deserve savage punishment. The dishonesty of news reporting is now so prevalent that a parent being told that their child was going into journalism should react in the same way as if being told their child was going into prostitution.

An example of the BBC seeking to ensure low self-esteem by the British Public was their treatment of the 200th year anniversary of Wilberforce's epic Act of Parliament, which effectively ended world-wide slavery. The BBC believes we should be using this anniversary to apologise for our role in slaving in the preceding centuries. The reality is of course that we should be celebrating our nation's unique role in the ending of slavery. Slavery had existed in all stages of mans development and had been part of every civilisation prior to the emergence of the ASG. Modern media seek to create the opinion that slavery is unique to Africans. The reality is that for almost two million years slaves were generally from European or Asian stock. In comparison Sub Saharan African slavery was a phenomenon, which lasted only 200/300 years. When the Wilberforce Act came into being, it did so at a time when the British Navy was omnipotent on all oceans. This meant that British ships were empowered to stop, search and free any slaves held in the ships of any Navy of any country in the world. This action cut of the flow of slaves to America and effectively created the economic conditions, which led to the universal abandonment of slavery. All Britons should be immensely proud that their Parliament had the courage to end a practice, which was as long as all human history. All Britons however should be aware of the BBC's role in seeking to denigrate this unique Act of Parliament, which ended world slavery.

The BBC, influence, quite deliberately, public opinion by presenting skewed or distorted portrayals of evolutionary group performance in misleading context, thus many programmes will suggest a large percentage of minority group senior manager or officer presence than is actually correct. Programmes centred on say, the Police, will very often present an Afro Caribbean personality filling the senior and most intellectually demanding management function within the portrayed episode. These personalities will represent a greater percentage on the screen than in real life.

Whilst there are many instances of skewed racial description within the BBC, Parliament has enthusiastically helped the process of misinformation. For instance crime statistics can not be presented by ethnic group, because the government is aware that such a presentation would identify clearly that a disproportionate number of criminal activities are committed by these groups within the major British city areas.

This skewed presentation is so misleading that should an individual, a stranger to Europe; land in England and decided to familiarise himself with this new country by watching television, he would be left with the clear impression that the UK was a majority Afro Caribbean/ Asian nation.

The reader should be aware that both in the press and in broadcasting the truth is missing. When you are watching the pretty announcer picked for the size of her mammary glands or her ethnicity rather than any intellectual ability, recognise that you are watching a charade, a nursing of public opinion rather than any attempt to honestly inform. When she gives you a dazzling smile as she reports the deaths of half a million people by some natural disaster forgive her, she is not paid to think, only to say what is written. Malevolent individuals with an agenda which has little to do with the prosperity or well being of this country, manipulate the news and opinion forming forums.

Remember always that the UK is not a multicultural nation; it is a nation of Anglo-Saxon, Celtic people who are also

Christian. Anyone who does not fit that profile is a stranger and ought to behave like one and ought to be treated like one.

As we are badly served by the press, so it is with our politicians, lacking vision or commitment to vision or principle, our current politicians are almost without exception, utterly irrelevant in the pages of history.

The phenomenon of the over civilised is a product of our own success. These are people who are raised in a society of care and in significant safety but who are not intelligent or educated enough to understand where that care and safety came from. They can not conceive of a society that does not behave in the way that their own behaves and are likely to attribute any deviant behaviour of other society's to current issues of supply or support. These people are incredibly dangerous and sometimes their innocence magnifies their danger. The over-civilised together with the Evil press have created an enormous problem for the ASG.

The behaviour of the scribbling classes or should I call them journalists, following the UK vote to leave the EU has given us an example of near treasonable behaviour. In addition peripheral politicians like Clegg and Fallon have behaved in a manner that should land them in prison.

PART 2

Part one of this book illustrated the hollow stupidity of political correctness and also showed the dreadful futures which may result. This treatise illustrates those actions which need to be put in place to combat this awful future.

These pages are written as an outline of a true revolutionary manifesto with no commitments to either the capitalist or socialist theories. The needs of the people require that the appropriate action whether from one or other of the philosophies will be adopted. Thus if an industry or organ of supply is better operated by direct nationalization then so be it, but if private enterprise is the efficient means of supply then that is the tool that the revolution will use.

Britain as a nation is threatened by both the end of the age of oil and the evolutionary destruction of its identity as a result of uncontrolled immigration. To survive these threats means that the British must engage in a social and political revolution of the most vigorous order. Some of the necessary actions to ensure our survival are set out hereunder.

The utter mediocrity of British politicians since the Second World War is the only consistent factor in British politics in that time, perhaps with the single exception of Mrs. Thatcher. In some cases this mediocrity has simply gently eased Britain from a global dominating force to an almost second rate power and in some cases this mediocrity coupled with malevolence has drastically accelerated that process. For instance in this second category, the government of Harold Wilson in its short life did more damage to Britain and its economy than all of the German bombing between 1939 and 1945. The British party system; which has aligned voters not in pursuit of representational excellence but rather in support of class labels is largely to blame for this phenomenon. The reality is that the

British Labour Movement whilst loyally supported by the working class has betrayed the working classes and taken that great social movement for change and given it the image of a cringing, whining, grubby little socialist with begging bowl in hand, envious of wealth and jealous of achievement. This destructive philosophy must itself be utterly destroyed. The Conservative Movement has simply betrayed the historical destiny of Britain.

The general population of England has common priorities in such matters as Education, Medicine, Law and Order, Crime and Punishment and Morality. The solutions to these concerns will not be found by a system that suggests that the needs of the working class will always be in opposition to the needs of the provision of capital. In the following pages we set out directional thoughts on these matters. The tone of these notes sets the scene for all the general changes that are necessary to rescue England from the current morass of mindless political correctness. This section ends with a clear statement in respect of 'Law' 'Morality' and 'Human rights' These abused terms have first to be put into their true perspective as simply tools of mans society with no actual natural substance.

Unless the outlines suggested in this document are implemented then Great Britain will continue on an accelerating decline into a multicultural disaster and become an unheeded member of the world community.

MANIFESTO OF THE ENGLISH REVOLUTION

As a direct result of the measures contained in this treatise, one million unsuitable immigrants currently residing in the UK will leave the country in the first year of the revolutionary government.

CLAUSE ONE.
CONSTITUTIONAL CHANGE

1) The Monarch shall remain the Titular Head of State, but will delegate His/Her powers in all political meetings of Heads of State to the elected President. The Monarch shall retain all other privileges. (This proposed measure will be underlined by a referendum.)

2) The President shall be elected as Political Head of State and Commander in Chief of the armed forces by direct suffrage on a cycle of four years.

3) The House of Lords shall be abolished in its entirety, and replaced by an elected chamber. All ennoblement's enacted since January 1946 shall be annulled.

4) The Chamber replacing the House of Lords shall be called the House of Prefects .

5).A Prefectorial seat will represent three adjacent Parliamentary constituencies. Members of the nobility will be eligible to stand as candidates for election in either house.

6) Elections for the House of Prefects will be located at mid-term of the election for President and will be for a term of four years.

7) Under current conditions the House of Prefects will be made up of 101 members.

8) Serving members of the armed forces will elect one Prefect. A serving member of the armed forces may not stand as a candidate.

9) The House of Commons will be elected simultaneously with the Presidential Elections and will provide a

government for a fixed term of four years. The date of the next general election will be known on the first day of the incoming parliament.

10) The President shall be responsible for the creation of government and the appointment of Ministers from the elected ranks of both houses.

11) For a legislative bill to become law it will require majority support in both chambers. A proposed 'Bill' will be discussed and voted on in the Lower House prior to being submitted to the House of Prefects. Policy can be generated in the House of Prefects but is then submitted to the lower house.

12) ***The people and government of Great Britain do not recognise or accept rulings made in any Court other than the established British Courts.***

13) Legislation emanating from where ever which has not passed fully through both Houses of the British Parliament will not be recognised or acted upon in the United Kingdom.

CLAUSE ONE A.

Representation of the people.

1) A person elected to either House of Parliament will receive no remuneration during a period of office other than his Parliamentary salary.

2) Any person elected to either House shall on election surrender any directorships, sinecures, or any paid employment.

3) Any person elected to either House will on the day following election surrender all shares held by that person to a specially created investment company which will during the whole period of the individual's term of office, manage those shares on his behalf without reference to the individual.

4) The Investment Company so formed will be structured and managed by representatives from the top five investment houses in the UK.

5) Any person elected to either House who disposes of shares (held at the time of nomination for election as a member of either house) to a nominee or family member shall be guilty of a criminal act of corruption. Such persons will be deprived of their elected seat and will suffer a term of imprisonment.

6) The salary of a Member of Parliament will be fixed as the average salary received by the managing directors of fifty selected companies with turnover in excess of fifty million pounds

7) Members of Parliament will receive no general expenses to supplement salary except where travel is required to represent the government. Members representing constituencies situated further than thirty miles from Westminster will have a free accommodation provided in a purpose built accommodation block located in Westminster.

8) Rail travel to and from a member's Constituency and Westminster shall be provided free of charge. Vehicle expenses will be paid between the home address and Westminster.

10) Service men and women in the armed forces will not vote in a particular Parliamentary constituency. All three

branches of the armed services, Royal Navy, Royal Air Force and Army, will elect an additional three members of Parliament. The nine elected members for the serviceman representation will not be serving personnel. No serving member of the armed forces will be eligible to stand for the military constituency.

CLAUSE 1b) ELECTORAL ELIGIBILITY

1) No person shall be eligible to vote in a general election who has not achieved the age of eighteen years, prior to the date of the declaration of that election. This provision does not include military service personnel.

2) Any person registering in order to vote for the first time shall be required to pass a simple literacy test

CLAUSE 1c) ELECTION PROCEDURE.

1) General elections and Presidential elections will be held on the fourteenth of October (Founder's Day) or the nearest Friday to the fourteenth of October.

2) No person shall be eligible to seek election to the Lower House below the age of twenty-one at the time of nomination.

3) No person shall be eligible to seek election to the Upper House who is below the age of thirty at the time of an election being declared.

4) All persons eligible to vote in a parliamentary election shall be required to exercise that vote unless medical

evidence is produced to support absence. It shall be deemed a criminal act to frustrate this order.

5) Party nomenclature may not be included on ballot papers. It is the responsibility of the voter to establish the identity of their preferred candidate.

6) Election booths will be electronically operated and end of poll count will be calculated by computer. Spoiled votes are not possible with electronic voting.

7) Parliamentary elections will be by single first past the post vote.

8) An election result will be known within one hour of closure of polls.

9) In the extremely unlikely event of a dead heat emerging from an electronic poll then that poll will be declared invalid and a fresh poll will be taken for that constituency one week later than the official election date.

10) Successful incoming candidates will take office on the First day of November following the date of the poll.

11) The Falkland Islands and Gibraltar will be designated as county authorities and will enjoy the full status of UK identity. Each will return a Prefect and a House of Commons member.

CLAUSE TWO:-
NATIONALITY

All persons resident in the British Isles shall be required to carry an identity card. An identity card simply carries the bearers name and National insurance number, home address and card number. Identity cards will be issued in three different formats. As will passports.

a) Full citizen.

b) Resident Alien

c) Temporary Resident.

2) **Class One Passport and Identity Card.**
A full citizen shall be able to prove Evolutionary Level One or Level Two ancestries (as defined by the Part One of this treatise) for a minimum of three generations on either Maternal or Paternal lineage.

.

Resident Alien.
A Resident Alien shall be a person unable to fulfil 2) but with three generations residential qualification on both Paternal and Maternal lineage. Such persons must retain the passport of their country of origin.

5) A holder of a Class One Identity Card will be entitled to vote or stand as a candidate in any British election, whether for National or Local Elections. A holder of a Class One Identity Card will be entitled and required to serve on a jury and will be entitled absolutely to be heard in any personal trial by a jury of Class One Identity Card holders.

6) A holder of a Class Two Identity Card will be entitled to vote in any British local election but will not be entitled to stand as a candidate in National elections. Nor will he/she be eligible to serve on a jury in the trial of a Class One, Cardholder. He/She must carry the passport from their country of origin.

7) The holder of any level of Identity card may be co-opted to serve on any level of government, except cabinet rank.

8) The holder of a Class Three Identity card may not hold executive office in Government, the Armed Forces or Police, nor may they vote in either local or national elections. He/She must carry the passport from their country of origin.

9) New residence in the UK is not permitted for any member of a level three or lower evolutionary group. (As defined by Part One of this treatise). Any persons currently legally residing in the UK whose place of birth or ancestry was in a level three or lower evolutionary racial group or country, as defined in Part One, may be in certain conditions permitted to remain in the UK. Such persons will not be entitled to a British passport. Such residents must retain the status and passport of their original country. Excluded from this order are any members of those communities who have served in any of the British armed forces, or in the police or who have in any way represented Britain in any International forum whether sporting or political. Such persons shall have discretional level one citizenship.

10) It shall be an offence for any person to attempt to enter Great Britain unless possessing a valid visa (or Passport in the case of EU residents) issued by the British Government or H.M Embassies. Carrier companies, whether Air Sea or Rail, allowing passage to persons not possessing a valid visa or Passport will be fined a standard fine of £100,000 on the first occasion and be required to provide return transport for the offender on the same day as attempted entry. A similar fine will be levied on a subsequent occasion and in addition a final warning to the company concerned will also be issued. If a third occasion of

unlawful entry is attributed to the carrier then the carrier will lose the right to provide entry services of any kind into the UK for a specified period.

CLAUSE THREE:-

LAW AND ORDER –CRIME AND PUNISHMENT.

All humans respond to reward and punishment in predicable ways and the following rules will provide a safe, progressive and healthy society. These measures include the reintroduction of the death penalty for a number of crimes and to respond to the entirely predictable liberal response, I would comment on the death sentence in the following manner.

a) **Liberal Augment. Capital punishment does not act as a deterrent**. This premise is arguable but irrelevant; the purpose of the death penalty is not designed to act as a deterrent.

b) **Liberal Augment. Capital punishment is revenge**. Again, arguable but irrelevant, no doubt grieving relatives of victims will always regard the death penalty as revenge but again that is not the purpose of reintroduction.

c) **The reason for the reintroduction of the Death Penalty.** ***Capital punishment is simply the only appropriate penalty for anyone who deliberately takes the gift of life from any other person.***

POLICING A SAFE SOCIETY

Within the first year of office the revolutionary government will publish a new Police Powers Bill aimed at restoring effective law enforcement. Crime will be halved in the UK within the first eighteen months of the RG administration.

1) Police Authorities will be synonymous with County borders. The Watch Committee for each county will be drawn from all Council Groups within a county authority.

3) The Chairman of a watch committee shall be a full time elected officer whose appointment will be achieved at the time of county authority elections. The chairman of a watch committee shall be known as the Police Executive Officer.

4) The Chief Constable of a Police Authority will report directly to a sub committee of the Home Office.

5) Special Branch will be detached from the control of local Police Authorities and become a National Organisation reporting to a newly created Department of National Security, which will also encompass the Intelligence Services. A full Cabinet member will head the Department of National Security.

6) All Police officers will carry a firearm with the strictest rules of engagement.

Changes to arrest and charge procedures.

1) A person may be arrested and taken for questioning to the local Police station where the arresting officer believes there is sufficient evidence of an offence to warrant arrest. An arrested person may be detained for twenty-four hours without charge where a senior officer of not less than Superintendent rank believes that a chargeable offence is likely to be proven.

2) Prior to arrest a person questioned by the Police in connection with an offence must answer reasonable questions put to them by the Officer concerned. **A person may not refuse to be questioned by the Police** or deny property access to a police officer making enquiries. If a search of such property is required, then

a search warrant is necessary as at present. A refusal to answer questions at this stage is an offence and will result in arrest. Following arrest in any circumstances, a person must not be asked questions by police officers except in the presence of his legal representative. If the individual concerned has no accredited legal representative then a lawyer must be provided whether or not the arrested individual requests representation.

3) A person arrested must be cautioned at the time of arrest by the use of the following words. "I am arresting you on suspicion of being involved in an offence of……. I must caution you that anything you say will be taken down in writing or may be electronically recorded and may be used against you in any subsequent trial.

NB. (The current caution in use is politically correct nonsense and adds nothing either to protection of the arrested person or to the police investigation.)

Change to rules of evidence.

Irrefutable evidence pertinent to establishing guilt or innocence ***however*** obtained will be allowable in court. Notwithstanding this, a person obtaining evidence by illegal means will be prosecuted with an offence of perverting the course of justice.

The general provisions outlined above do not apply where the alleged offender is accused of terrorist activities.

THE TERRORIST DECLARATION.

1) The definition of a terrorist shall be an individual, a group of individuals, an organisation or number of organisations who seek to influence, damage or change a democratically elected government by means of violence.

2) A terrorist is further defined as a person who carries out acts of violence against persons or property in support of ideological or political motives.

3) In those circumstances where the Department of National Security believe an act of terrorism is being planned or has taken place, then any individual reasonably identified as being concerned in those matters in any way may be arrested and detained for seven days without charge.

4) The caution used in respect of a terrorist suspect is as follows: - I am arresting you on suspicion of being involved in terrorist activities. I caution you that as a terrorist suspect you ***do not have a right to silence*** but must answer truthfully any questions put to you by the police. Anything you say will be taken down in writing or electronically recorded and may be used in any subsequent trial.

5) A terrorist suspect on arrest will be taken to a special terrorist holding centre where at this stage the arrested person may nominate a legal representative or alternatively one will be provided by the State.

6) The Crown Prosecution Service will not evaluate evidence of terrorist activity. Consideration of prosecutable worth will be made by a special Terror Prosecution Service.

7) When after consideration of the evidence available, the TPS establish that a prosecution is right and proper, then the status of the terrorist suspect changes. The terrorist now becomes an 'Outlaw' in the ancient sense of the word. By his established intent he/she has signalled that he/she does not accept the rule of law provided by the properly and democratically elected government he seeks to attack and therefore ***he/she has no right to expect the same protection offered by that government to its law abiding citizens.*** The suspect now surrenders

any right to private consultation with his legal representative, and no longer has the protection of the right to avoid self-incrimination. He/she must answer ***truthfully all questions*** put to him and where he/she refuses to answer any question then the assumption will be that an answer would incriminate.

8) The trial of a charged Terrorist suspect will be before a jury made up of one High Court Judge (retired) one Chief Constable (retired) and ten lay jurors.

9) A person convicted of a terrorist offence shall suffer death by hanging. Such a person shall have the same right of appeal as any other condemned person.

CORRUPTION

DEFINITION OF THE CRIME OF CORRUPTION

The crime of corruption shall be deemed to have been committed when a person or an official in any capacity whatsoever deliberately arrange events, services or duties in such a way as to enhance their own wealth or prestige or reputation to the disadvantage of their client, customer or any member of the general public and contrary to the accepted responsibilities, rules or duties of the occupation or service that they are engaged in performing or supplying.

1) If a Judge, Lawyer, Court Official or elected Member of Parliament is convicted of an act of, or a conspiracy in an act of corruption, then they shall serve a custodial sentence of not less than ten years hard labour.

2) If a Policeman, Prison Officer, Bank Official, Company Director, School Teacher or Local Government Officer is convicted of an act of, or conspiracy in an act of corruption, they shall be imprisoned for a minimum of five years hard labour.

VIOLENCE

Definition of murder.

The unlawful killing of an individual will be classified as murder when there is acceptable proof that the aggressor intended that the victim should be killed. Among acceptable proofs of the intention to kill, is the carrying of a knife or firearm in a public place where the carrier commits an act of murder. Payment of an individual to secure the death of a person shall also be considered as proof of intention to kill, as is the acceptance of such a payment.

1) If a person or persons are convicted of an act of murder during an unlawful sex act, or of a conspiracy in such an act of murder then that person or those persons shall suffer death by hanging.

2) If a person or persons are convicted of the murder of a child during an event of kidnapping, or of conspiracy in such an act of murder then that person or persons shall suffer death by hanging.

3) If a person or persons are convicted of the murder of a child during a responsibility of care and protection, or of conspiracy in such an act of murder then that person or persons shall suffer death by hanging.

4) If a person or persons are convicted of an act of murder during their involvement in an act of robbery then that person or persons shall suffer death by hanging.

5) If a person or persons plan the murder of an individual for motives of greed, envy enmity or hatred then that person or persons shall suffer death by hanging.

6) If a male person between the age of 16 and 21 is convicted of an assault occasioning actual bodily harm then that person shall serve a minimum of two years in a military penal regiment. If a person sent to a penal regiment under this provision absconds they shall receive five years hard labour as an alternative sentence.

7) If a female person between the ages of 16 and 21 is convicted of an assault occasioning actual bodily harm them that person shall serve a minimum of one year in a military penal regiment.

8) If a person occasion the death of a person as a consequence of marital betrayal then providing the accused had no knowledge of the betrayal prior to the critical act of violence then this crime will be classified as a crime of passion and will be punished by imprisonment.

9) **If** a person occasion the death of a person for whatever reason with malice aforethought and planning designed to bring about that death then that person shall suffer death by hanging.

10) A defence of Unfit to Plead shall not be recognised as sufficient to avoid penalty. In such a case, evidence establishing guilt or innocence in responsibility for the unlawful killing in question shall remain the only criteria on which a penalty will be enforced.

11) **The penalty of death shall only be carried out where there is conclusive forensic evidence to support other evidence. Where conviction is secured through witness or other evidence but not supported by forensic evidence then the guilty party will suffer life imprisonment. Life imprisonment in this context means whole of life custody.**

12) A condemned person awaiting execution is allowed one appeal against sentence. The appeal must take place

within one month of sentence and is allowable on only two grounds.

APPEAL GROUNDS.

1) The production of new evidence not previously available. Such evidence must be clearly pertinent to establish innocence.

2) Evidence that the trial at which the sentence was established was improperly conducted and as a consequence the verdict was unsafe.

3) Evidence brought to support an application under clauses 1) and 2) above shall be considered at a pre-retrial hearing to determine validity.

4) English Law will also provide for a Not Proven verdict which juries may decide upon. In such cases where such a verdict is determined, then on the production of further and better evidence a new trial may be held.

PUBLIC DEMONSTRATIONS.

It has been a mainstream of British freedom that any group can demonstrate their objections to a government policy or indeed to any matter of public concern. This right must be protected, but the use of this right to generate public disorder common recently will end with the publication of a new Public Order Act. Under the New Act any body wishing to conduct a protest march or demonstration may do so providing they agree a route for the demonstration with the appropriate police authority. The route will be escorted by a police presence. In those circumstances where a demonstrator breaks through the police cordon then it will be deemed that an act of riot has occurred by the individuals concerned.. In revolutionary Britain any incident of riot carries a mandatory penalty of one to five years Hard Labour.

CLAUSE FOUR:-

EDUCATION.

The purpose of education is not to satisfy the selfish desire to acquire status or wealth, nor is education the gift of any one person. Education is the States recognition that its people must be, and have a right to be, equipped to compete intellectually at all levels within both local society and international society and to contribute to the general welfare of the society that gave them birth. The State provides free education in order that any individual may achieve the highest possible exercise of his/her intellect. The State expects that in return the individual will use that expertise where possible in the service of the people. There is no conflict between this need and the opportunity to achieve the 'good' life by improved earning power.

It is the right of all persons of whatever evolutionary level, to receive a free education, sufficient to achieve the maximum standard of attainment possible from his or her intellectual ability. The current fashion to remove progress by exam is rejected. It is certain that the hurdle of exam is typical of the hurdles a child will face when seeking to succeed in the adult world. Competition in sport or academic subjects is desirable and an individual has to come to terms with coming second sometimes.

The structure of education in ASG Britain will be as follows:

1) **A** standard Educational Authority will be based in each British County and it will be their responsibility to provide the educational structure to fulfil the programme here set out.

2) **B**etween the ages of five and ten years a child will receive an education in primary schools which are primarily designed to achieve literacy and numeracy (L&N). To this end not less than 70% of attendance time in this period will be occupied with L&N.

3) **A**t the age of eleven, all children will be assessed by exam and separated into fast track and standard track tuition. Fast track children will attend special schools designed to achieve University entry as standard. By yearly exam, children unable to perform within the fast track system will be removed to standard track. Standard track schools will employ streaming, with more gifted children being given the opportunity to transfer to a fast track school by yearly exam.

4) At the age of thirteen years, children in Standard Stream schools will be able to qualify for Technical or Trade collages. It is expected that the number of places for fast track tuition shall be equal to twenty five percent of the juvenile population.

A strictly controlled system of corporal punishment will be applied to all violent or disruptive male students between the ages of eleven and sixteen. Each school shall employ a licensed janitor or janitors for this purpose.

4) Male students judged to be incapable of further intellectual advancement within the school system may choose to leave full time education on attaining the age of fifteen.

5) Entry into University will be achieved by Matriculation. Matriculation in this context means achieving not less than 'B' grade in six academic subjects at the end of sixth form collage.

6) Free attendance at University will be available to all citizens in any Science or Engineering related course together with Language, Law, History, Geography and related subjects. Esoteric subjects like Art, Music and general studies will receive no Government support of any kind. It is expected that those industries that utilise these subject studies will provide either the financial or the educational infrastructure to produce these skill requirements. Tax structures to enable companies to achieve this objective will be part of the revised Tax structure. Education is the gift of society and the cost of education is directed at achieving sustainable intellectual growth and socially valued and developing infrastructure. There is clear evidence that socially sponsored education, which is irrelevant to the needs of the majority, encourages a decline in academic standards. Such subjects as General Studies, American studies and similar non-functional subjects are simply public money consumers. A list of those subjects qualifying for free University entry is contained separately. Similarly a list of those subjects currently qualifying which will be removed from the approved list is contained separately.

7) A student attending University will receive a cost of living allowance and will have free access to transport in pursuit of his/her studies.

8) The present expensive and unnecessary system of farming students around the country to obtain their qualifications will be abolished. A student will attend his local County University and reside in his/her home address. A student will receive a cost of living allowance and will enjoy free travel to the local University. An individual who successfully achieves matriculation will be **guaranteed** a place in University. In those counties where a University does not exist, a new standard format establishment will be built. Existing Universities with narrow syllabus conditions will be required to broaden their programme to fulfil the general subject need. There is a need to recognise a number of Universities who have had a special and historically significant role in British History. Universities such as Oxford Cambridge Durham Edinburgh will continue to select candidates on a separate methodology. (There are more than four Universities in this category.)

9) All senior schools must have access to playing fields in order that all of the national sport forms may be engaged in

CLAUSE FIVE:- SEXUAL & SOCIAL MORALITY

Not included in this publication.

CLAUSE SIX:-
THE MANAGEMENT OF MEDIA.

1) **A** free press is part of the West's tradition and must be maintained. However the term 'Free Press' must not be allowed to licence corruption, malice or treason.

2) **A**n instrument of media is defined as a newspaper, a radio or television broadcasting station or a web-site or any medium of communication seeking the attention of the general public.

3) **T**he head of any instrument of media information shall only be allowed to operate as such within the United Kingdom, if ***licensed*** to perform such a function. That license will normally be granted to Class One citizens who fulfil all reasonable conditions.

4) **A** person licensed to operate in control of an instrument of media information will be ***personally*** responsible for the payment of any damages awarded in a case of libel successfully brought against his or her instrument. It will be a legal standard that an award in libel against an instrument of media shall be not less than two million pounds.

5) **I**t shall be an act of criminal conspiracy for any third party to provide funds to a licensed operative who is required to fulfil the terms of this order (4)

6) Where an instrument of media information seeks to use a public survey to illustrate any aspect of opinion or forecast, such a survey may not be used unless it fulfils the minimal statistical standard of a Mori poll. It shall be a criminal offence to use any survey not fulfilling this directive.

7) Any instrument of media information seeking to predict forward events in political or financial matters may not use the words ‘Might’ ‘May’ or ‘Could’ in any such prediction.

The BBC will be broken into four separate Corporations, Television News, Sport and Entertainment Broadcasting, Radio broadcasting and World News service. The BBC will be purged from top to bottom to remove anti British bias and many executives currently employed in this broadcasting service will face serious criminal proceedings.

BBC Television Broadcasting will be permitted to carry a ten-minute per hour slot of commercial advertising within its programmes.

As a consequence of activities over recent years, many BBC executives will be charged with actively participating in the following offences. If found guilty of these charges severe custodial sentences will result.

1) Conspiracy to promote and support the creation of multi-culturism against the wishes and to the disadvantage of the historical British population.

2) Conspiracy to damage British Business by negative and damaging editorial, reporting and presentation.

3) Conspiracy to portray British History in a negative and dismissive manner encouraging a downgraded view of British achievements.

CLAUSE SEVEN: HEALTH CARE

The objective of the NHS is to provide health care at the point of request for all normal sickness conditions. NHS responsibility for sick care ends when the cost of such care exceeds an established upper limit. In particular 'no cure conditions' can not be supported by the NHS. A person entering into a condition which means care without foreseeable end, must receive such care by a different mechanism.

The NHS has been used for a political football by all political parties and the augments used are thoroughly immoral. It is suggested by an unending stream of commentators from the right and from the left that all we have to do is pour more and more money into the NHS and all will be well, this philosophy is absolutely wrong

It is vitally necessary for people to understand that the size of the NHS budget is not limitless and that at a certain level of cost, care will not be provided.

For instance we might use the following definition of care required outside the NHS scope, if the care required by an individual has an annualised cost greater than the average national wage then this level of care can not be provided by the NHS.

The revolutionary government will contract with a number of insurers to fund those care costs unsupportable by the ordinary NHS. Care in this category which is outside the scope of NHS funding will be provided by an insurance fund which all taxpayers contribute to.

All individuals will have an additional monthly contribution added to the National Insurance stamp. This sum will be invested in an insurance company or a number of insurance companies. This insurance policy must be drawn on when treatment cost exceeds the norm for the NHS.

It shall be a criminal offence for anyone to take strike action or encourage strike action by any medical practitioner at any level. Such an offence will carry a mandatory term of five years hard labour.

1) Free medicine and medical treatment will be provided for all persons irrespective of evolutionary source.

2) Health care will be organised by County authorities who have a responsibility to provide a full range of facilities and mechanism's. A County Medical Authority (CMA) will be headed by a full time professional who will chair and direct an enabling committee. It is the CMA's responsibility to ensure that there are sufficient hospital beds available at all times to cater for normal statistical need. In any given population there are a calculable number of bed hours, which are required to minister to general ill health. It is the CMA's responsibility in each county to establish this number and to provide hospital accommodation to fulfil that need. In-house medical care for long term sick (Over three day's) (LTS) patients will take place in generally specialised hospitals of significant size. The size of these institutions will be established by professional analysis. This exercise is designed to calculate cost/efficiency/size for maximum units that will be required. The CCGHU (Central County General Hospital Unit) units will act as a central collection point of LTS from Smaller Community Units (Similar to Cottage Hospitals of former establishment) strategically located throughout the county to provide accident, outpatient and short term accommodation services.

3) The CCGHU units will provide the most sophisticated and up to date operational techniques that exist at that time. All

target systems in respect of operation and attendance times will be discontinued

4) The County Enabling Committee will include representatives from CCGHU and SCUs and will be responsible for monitoring efficiency and ensuring progression in introducing latest medical techniques and treatments.

5) The CMA is responsible for managing the total medical taxation budget for the population within its boundaries. Apart from normal National Insurance contributions from central government, a CMA is authorised to collect a local medical tax from both employee and employer. This tax is described annually and is subject to government oversight.

6) Across the country, eight regional centres of excellence (RCE) will be established to provide the specialist medical care for advanced medical conditions such as cancer and other potentially terminal diseases. These RCE's will also house research and training facilities for medical practitioners and surgeons.

8) A National University and research facility will be established for the sole purpose of genetic research. It is probable that the solutions to the many serious medical conditions, which afflict mankind, will be found within this research facility. The recruitment of students for this newly established University will of necessity be by a different route to other universities

CLAUSE EIGHT:-
FINANCIAL RESPONSIBILITY

1) Remuneration received by any person shall generate a personal opportunity to obtain credit or attain loans up to a calculable figure based on a fixed multiplication of that remuneration. The providers of remuneration will be required to provide a certification of that gross remuneration to each employee. Credit or any form of loan granted to any individual in excess of accepted certificated income multiplier ***shall not be recoverable in law***.

2) In those circumstances where due to ill health, loss of employment or other special circumstance an individual or family are unable to service a properly obtained mortgage on a domestic property then the local authority in which the property is located shall be obliged to purchase the property concerned and allow the occupants to remain in that property as tenants. This action is prescribed where the mortgage owners of their free will opt for this clause rather than exercise their right to sell the property on the open market. In purchasing the property the authority will only be required to discharge the outstanding mortgage balance.

3) The property concerned shall be held by the authority in fief for the former owner pending two events.

a) The former owner recovers full income capability and is able to resume ordinary mortgage payments. The provider of the original mortgage shall as a duty provide a new facility to the recovered owner reflecting that term of years and balance outstanding at the time of original crisis.

b) The death of the former owner preceding recovery shall empower the authority to sell the property for ***full market*** value. The proceeds of such a sale will firstly reimburse the authority for expenses accrued and secondly, remaining value shall be added to the deceased's estate.

4) If the former owner abandons the tenancy then the authority shall be empowered to sell the property.

5) **Power of bailiff.** If a provider of goods or services employ a bailiff to recover costs of a failed agreement then the bailiff shall only be empowered under law to recover those goods provided by that person or institution. Goods seized under this provision must be sold at full market value. It shall be a criminal offence for a bailiff to remove goods which were not made available by the frustrated agreement.

6) Any person experiencing serious debt through unavoidable changes in income availability occasioned by such things as unemployment, sickness or other unavoidable events may apply for a Reconstruction Order from a specially created Court. The Court will when granting an order :-

a) Freeze all interest on debts being experienced by the debtor.

b) Amortise the total indebtedness into a single sum.

c) Fix a monthly payment figure achievable by the debtor and allocate this figure on a proportional basis to all creditors.

These arrangements do not include mortgage debt, which is dealt with elsewhere.

7) The figure of debt where a creditor may apply for a compulsory bankruptcy petition is raised to £20.000. An application for a bankruptcy petition may not be entered into where a Reconstruction Order is being considered.

8) An individual may personally apply for a bankruptcy order at the lower sum of £10.000.

The revolutionary government will encourage the traditional desire of UK citizens to purchase their own home and to this end the following provisions will apply.

9) Mortgage interest relief will be reintroduced for all domestic home purchases under the figure of £500.000. This order will apply only to a single residential home.

10) Inheritance tax will be abolished for all estates worth less than £5.000.000.

CLAUSE EIGHT (a)

The provision of social benefits is a ***privilege not a right***. In the first instance this privilege will be extended only to those persons who carry a class one identity card.

Any person whose place of birth and ancestry is outside the definition of a level one or two homeland as defined in the LBB, is eligible for **one form of benefit only.** Such a person requiring benefit from the State will be provided with a fully funded transportation ticket to their original homeland. A resettlement allowance of £1000 may also be applied for where this provision is being applied.

Any person from a non ASG background who is found guilty of a crime under United Kingdom criminal law, will on the day of conviction be deported to their ancestral homeland. Such persons will not be eligible for the payment of a resettlement grant. Excluded from this order are persons convicted of the crime of murder. Such persons on conviction are subject to the established legal penalty.

Any person claiming asylum status as a consequence of persecution may only be admitted to the UK where definitive proof of the existence of an arrest warrant in the refugee's nation of origin is provided. Additionally a refugee may only claim sanctuary in the UK where definitive proof exists that the UK was the first place of entry after homeland flight.

The revolutionary government will examine benefit payments carefully and remove the burden from the taxpayer those payments properly belonging elsewhere. For instance in the case of an unmarried mother, the responsibility for financing that child does not belong to the State, the responsibility belongs to the person who fathered the child. Law will be introduced which will mean that in no circumstance can the father avoid payment.

MILITARY SECURITY

CLAUSE NINE:-

Any legal company having taken part in the prosecution of British service veterans will be prohibited from practice within the UK and individual lawyers or barristers having acted in these affairs will be unable to practice in the UK. In cases where practices have made a deliberate attempt to create such prosecutions then those individuals or practices will be subject to a new law making the prosecution of service personnel Exclusive to the domain of a special military legal department. Prosecution by any other means is unlawful and punishable by imprisonment

In the interests of the security of the British people it is the responsibility of its government to ensure that our military capability stays at the highest level of technological requirement at all times. Cost is not, and can never be, a consideration in the fulfilment of this clause.

1) All male citizens of the UK will be required to serve two years military service under a new National Service Act. All women citizens of the UK will be required to serve for one year under the National Service Act.

2) Any person avoiding National Service for other than genuine medical incapacity grounds will not be permitted to seek election to government positions or to hold a majority share holding in any British Company.

3) Conscientious objectors shall be required to serve in non-combatant roles in nursing or catering. Refusal to serve in these circumstances will result in a sentence of hard labour for an equivalent period.

In an age where the most worthless of human debris can use a portable device to inflict death and destruction on an individual or a number of individuals it is necessary to change the centuries long conventions in respect of the management of occupied territory and the conduct of localised wars.

It is no longer possible to consider all civilians in an occupied territory as 'innocent' and to seek equable administration of such persons. On the basis of a belief that occupation of any foreign territory will only be the result of a reaction to a threat to our own national security or economic benefit, then all residents of a nation issuing such a threat must of necessity be treated as uniformly hostile to our interests.

It cannot be accepted that British troops engaged in the peaceful administration of a geographical area, are subjected to continuous attack by persons hiding in the body of any population. Nor can administration be effective where low intelligence suicide bombers are employed. In these circumstances the whole population must be considered as hostile.

If a member of a terrorist organisation brings down death on innocent British individuals then they must understand that the consequences are terrible and unendurable.

In this time we enter into the age of the technological army.

The B.R.G. will double the number of nuclear submarines in active service.

The RAF will be restored to a full operational service as a matter of priority.

The Royal Navy will be restored by a significant building programme to effective capability as a class one priority.

A NEW MODEL ARMY

The traditional organisation of regiments and divisions is here abolished.

The organisational structure of the army will be based on a Legion. A Legion will comprise five thousand men; each Legion is divided into five cohorts, each of one thousand men. A cohort is divided into ten centuries and each century into five companies.

Four of the cohorts are combat personnel; the fifth is the Drone Control and service cohort.

Ten Legions comprise a battlefield army.

A Company is commanded by a Lieutenant
A Century is commanded by a Captain
A Cohort is commanded by a Major
A Legion is commanded by a Colonel.

A combat cohort has a permanent establishment of two drones attached. The Cohorts will bear the names and colours of the traditional regiments. In addition the Drone control Cohort has a wide range of drone capability from miniature to medium size destructive capability.

Normal transport for a Cohort is by helicarriers. A helicarrier is a light helicopter with no superstructure, with a central spine which carries ten men each side of that central spine.

A NEW MODEL NAVY

All navel action will be a fleet action.

A fleet will be established in the Atlantic, a second in the Mediterranean and a third in the Indian Ocean.

A fleet comprises of a 'King' ship, this is a new class of warship, being an aircraft carrier of some two hundred fifty thousand tons and bearing two flight decks. These carriers will be known as Battle Carriers.

A Battle carrier is escorted by eight Destroyers and One Missile Cruiser.

The fleet also possess two helicarriers; these vessels each carry a full Marine Commando Legion

All capital ships of the Royal Navy will be powered by nuclear engines

CLAUSE TEN.

TRADE UNIONS

It is essential for a successful British economy that its workplaces have within them a strong Trade Union organisation. In the absence of a strong trade union, working people will be open to abuse and will certainly be exploited.

1) Trade Union members must preserve the right to the withdrawal of labour subject to a secret ballot.

2) All companies employing more than 100 employees must practice full financial disclosure.

3) All annual agreements between organised labour and management must be contained in a document drawn with both parties' agreement by a legal practice. Such agreements will be enforceable in law.

4) Police, Teachers, Doctors, Nurses and Border Control officials may not engage in withdrawal of labour. An independent body drawn from Parliament, the Courts and from the associations representing the employees will administer their interests in terms of pay and conditions.

5) It shall be an offence punishable by imprisonment for any individual to foster or encourage a withdrawal of labour in any of the categories of employment contained in 4)

6) It shall be an offence punishable by imprisonment for any individual to foster or encourage a withdrawal of labour without a secret ballot.

7) It shall be an offence punishable in law for any member of management to seek to prevent the lawful operation of an elected union official from the performance of his duties.

8) No Parliamentary bill directly applicable to working conditions and safety at work practices will be put before Parliament without first having been discussed with a working committee of the TUC.

All Trade Union representatives shall on election attend a specially created collage for education in employment and safety at work legislation.

CLAUSE ELEVEN

THE EUROPEAN ECONOMIC COMMUNITY

This chapter was written before the referendum of May 2016.

Britain will leave the EEC on the first day of January following the election of the Revolutionary Government.

Membership of the EEC has been a major contributory factor in the decline of Britain. Incompetent politicians such as Edward Heath believed that joining the EEC would mean a bonanza for UK businesses. The facts are of course, that instead of Britain exploiting the European market, Britain has herself been exploited by the European manufacturers with the resultant elimination of major British employers and many jobs. In any debate about the benefits of EEC membership the question must always be asked, what are those benefits. Consider the following: -

1) Since joining the EEC the balance of trade between the EEC and the UK has moved in favour of the EEC by a very large percentage. The cost of this movement in jobs and profitable companies in Britain is incalculable.

2) Britain receives only a tiny percentage of its own contribution's back. The contributions made by Britain to the EEC would have provided a new hospital in every major British town or would have funded a significant part of our defence budget. Britain has been the provider of infrastructure, education and medicine to all of the poorer members of the Europe to the clear disadvantage of our own people.

3) A number of recent investigations have suggested that British membership of the EEC is costing the U.K. taxpayer between 80 and 100 ***Billion per annum.***

4) The single nation concept now being pursued by the EEC will be of benefit to most of Europe but not to Britain. There are no mature societies in Europe. Without exception each has grown out of comparatively recent social or military violence and generally survived only as a consequence of Anglo-American beneficence. None of them has a history of continual self-management over more than seventy years. On the other hand Britain has maintained a self-governing state for nine hundred and seventy three years (2009). The society created in that time is the most mature society on earth and can only be damaged by exposure to immature influences through the creation of this artificial state.

5) Every European (exception the German people) is a net debtor to the UK and every single taxpayer in the UK has carried on his back the burden of Europe since inception.

6) The Axis of power being created by the French and German governments is designed to sideline British international aspirations and to emasculate British International authority. This Axis is succeeding in its objectives and is being financed in its efforts by the British people.

7) When Britain ceases to contribute to Europe it is likely that the EEC will have significant funding problems.

8) Whilst British membership of the EEC continues, it is not possible to control the necessary investment in British industry essential to the creation of wealth creating industries. We are entirely at the mercy of foreign investors who have no vested interest in British success.

Britain will withdraw from the EEC on The first of January following achieving electoral power.

There are those who will maintain that British trade would be crippled by such an action. Consider the following:-

1) British trade with Europe has moved continuously in favour of Europe since membership first took place.

2) Britain represents one of the largest importers of German vehicles. Germany can not afford to lose that market and will engage in reciprocal trading arrangements.

3) Britain is one of the largest importers of French wine, agricultural and engineering products. France can-not afford to lose that market without severely damaging French employment and financial well being. Whilst not enjoying the experience the French will be forced to engage in reciprocal trading.

Added in December 2016-12-05

Mrs May's negotiation status is a simple one. She needs to declare that Britain will be prepared to offer tariff free entry by European countries to the British Market and expects Europe to reciprocate. Britain will allow full access by European Banks to the British Banking system and expects Europe to reciprocate.

On the Monday following the two year negotiating period after the operation of clause 50, Britain should arbitrarily impose these conditions on our own borders. And await response.

The minutia of the myriad interfaces requiring negotiation should be complete within the two years.

CLAUSE TWELVE

:

THE MANAGEMENT OF INDUSTRY.

1) Within one year of revolutionary government gaining power in Britain full employment will be experienced. Indeed as a consequence of other measures within this treatise a general shortage of labour will be experienced by year three. The revolutionary government will create a new Steel industry with the creation of fully automated steel production matching the best in world wide cost achievements. This new industry will be expected to produce all of the UK needs in Steel within a period of ten years. Direct investment by the government will provide the capital for these new industries.

2) On day one of executive power the revolutionary government will prohibit the registration of newly manufactured personal vehicles which cannot achieve a minimum petrol consumption of 100 miles per gallon. This order will take effect with new registrations occurring one year after the election of the revolutionary government. A new car industry providing Hybrid or full electric Engine cars will be created and very quickly all new cars registered in the UK will be required to be powered in this way. With Britain out of the EEC we will be able to control import volumes in the interest of British workers. It is anticipated that in a very short time most cars sold in the UK will be manufactured in this country. The revolutionary government will negotiate with the food producers outside the EEC on a reciprocal basis to achieve once again the cheap food policies of past years

10) It will be necessary for the revolutionary government to pursue a policy of initial direct investment designed to replace essential industries lost in the period of chaos since entry into the EEC.

Direct investment in the re-creation of Machine Tool Manufacture, In the case of the Machine Tool Industry, companies creating new machine tools will have a 75% reduction in all of its tax returns to encourage reestablishment of this critical industry. Steel Production and Aerospace projects are a priority.

Any company or person laying down a new machine tool company shall be free of business taxes for a period of ten years.

11) The government must ensure that the provision of all computer technology must be created in the UK and in particular the provision of a MicroChip producing industry is a class one priority.

12)

In the provision of items of infrastructure vital to the progress of the nation's prosperity. (Airport provision, extra runways, rail or road communication systems) the current method of public enquiry will be scrapped and an all party committee given final authority in authorising construction go ahead.

13)

Both Heathrow and Gatwick will be given an extra runway. In the first month of its existence the revolutionary government will autherise the construction of both runways and construction will start immediately. There will be no Public enquiry and both runways must be operational within three years.

The government will take into public ownership all Sea Ports, Air Ports and international Rail entries. There will be a completely new office of border control established to police these entry points.

Direct investment by the government is not aimed at creating more state-owned industries but is only a first step in creating companies who will be returned to shareholding management as soon as effective and profitable conditions have been created.

MEASURES TO MAXIMISE ENERGY SAVING

1) It shall be the governments aim to change all general electricity generation from fossil fuel to that provided by Nuclear energy. A construction programme to achieve this end will be established on week one of the revolutionary government. The target for full nuclear electricity generation will be the year 2050.

2) Personal motor vehicles newly registered in the UK on the second anniversary of the establishment of the revolutionary government must be capable of a minimum of 100 miles per gallon of fuel used

3) It shall be unlawful to heat domestic properties by the burning of oil. All existing installations shall remain lawful but a government programme to assist the conversion of such installations shall begin immediately.

4) All newly built domestic properties must have a provision for solar power heating of water.

5) All Navel Units above a declared tonnage, constructed after revolutionary day one (RD1) will be provided with nuclear engines for propulsion.

6) The rail system will be greatly extended, returning to service rural areas, which were excluded by the Beeching cuts.

7) The British coal mining industry will be reopened on a large scale with the objective of providing a new Coal Gas industry for domestic users.

8) The coasts of the United Kingdom possess some of the greatest tidal movements in the world. These tidal forces need to be harnessed as additional power generation.

CLAUSE THIRTEEN.

DUTIES OF A COUNTY AUTHORITY

The responsibilities of a County Authority in respect of Medicine, Education and Policing are covered earlier in this document. In addition to those already specified, a County Authority is required to provide services in many social areas. Some of the more important services are:-

1) Maintain existing road systems. To enable Authorities to perform this requirement more efficiently, the total of monies raised by road tax for vehicles registered in that county will be made available to the County Authority.

2) Each County Authority will be required to provide a Central Waste Disposal Unit (CWDU) capable of incinerating waste and providing a full recycling service. Each Authority must provide a once weekly waste collection service to its residents and all separation of recyclable waste must be performed at the CWDU.

3) In the performance of its demanded level of duties a County Authority may levy a local tax on all non-food purchases. (Excludes children's clothing and educational material).

4) All County Authorities are required to work for the provision of comprehensive sporting facilities for its youth population. A bi-annual programme of inter county competition is required on a mandatory basis to stimulate excellence. It is a mandatory requirement on all authorities to ensure that all children reach an adequate swimming standard by the age of thirteen.

5) It is the responsibility of a County Authority to ensure that any child attends his/her ***nearest*** school. This requirement applies to infant school junior school and senior school. A

successful University applicant will attend their local County University.

6) Provide adequate housing for low-income families. To this end the sale of council houses will end immediately. The local authority must purchase existing ex-council houses coming onto the property market. The local authority will pay an original purchaser the original purchase price plus the average housing price increase experienced over the period of ownership. People having purchased ex-council houses from original owners will be paid the market price of the property.

7) The provision of welfare benefits and the policing of child welfare are the responsibility of the County Authority and in particular the County Authority is required to provide an inspection authority for the policing of child welfare. In those circumstances where there is evidence or a suspicion of the maltreatment of any child, then the appointed school inspector shall have unrestricted, and unannounced right of access to that child. It shall be a criminal offence for any person to deny the right of access by the school inspector.

NB. The required provisions of Clause Fourteen are extremely complex. For a full guideline of County responsibilities under Clause Fourteen refer to the full explanatory guide to the revolution contained in the Little Blue Book part two.

Manchester City will build 200,000 council homes over a period of three years

Birmingham City will build 300,000 council homes over a period of three years

London will build two new suburbs of affordable housing over a period of five years.

In the construction of these new suburbs all consideration of green belt land will be set aside.

CLAUSE FOURTEEN

IMMIGRATION.

1) On day one of the revolutionary government **all** immigration into the United Kingdom will be prohibited for a period of six months. All immigration from non-ASG countries will be prohibited permanently. In this time an authority to ensure that limited immigration on the single basis of financial/skill need into the United Kingdom is established. Such inward immigration will be exclusively from ASG countries as defined by in Part one of this treatise.

2) Asylum will only be allowed where evidence exists that a warrant for arrest has been issued or is likely to be issued for the applicant and that additionally the entry into the United Kingdom is the first country entered after flight. Unauthorised entry into the UK will result in transportation of the illegal entry to their home country on the same day as entry.

3) All entry into the United Kingdom for other purposes will require a visa issued by the UK Department of Entry.

4) A carrier of any kind, by sea, air or rail, conveying a foreign national into the UK without an appropriate visa will incur a fine of One Million pounds and be required to transport such a person back to place of origin by return transport.

5) Any immigrant from a level three or below evolutionary group who has settled in the UK within the last five years and is in receipt of any form of State Benefit is required to leave the UK and return to the country of their origin within three months. Such persons are eligible to apply for the provision of an airline ticket and a £1000 resettlement grant.

CLAUSE FIFTEEN.

DIPLOMATIC IMMUNITY

Diplomatic immunity in the UK will be limited to the Ambassador and ten nominated persons. All embassy property (buildings) will retain diplomatic immunity, being considered as part of the territory of the country concerned.

A person employed within an embassy outside the nominated ten persons may be given temporary diplomatic status on application when delegated to carry diplomatic material. All other employees within an embassy are subject, outside the embassy, to the constraints of ordinary law.

CLAUSE SIXTEEN.
THE PROVISION OF FOREIGN AID.

The United Kingdom will not provide Cash Foreign Aid except in extremely special circumstances. Instead a system of direct aid will be employed.

Where a foreign government of slender resource requires the provision of services or infrastructure in the interest of its people and has convinced the British Government of that need. Then the UK will provide direct assistance in the form of goods or systems required which will be manufactured in the UK and will also provide direct labour employed by the British government to implement or install such aid.

The British Government will maintain a 200 bed prefabricated hospital and medical supplies, capable of air transport for deployment to any disaster area. Medical practitioners around the country may register for inclusion on the list of those needed in any such disaster. The hospital will contain full surgical operational facilities.

Law, Morality and Human Rights

Fact. In the natural order there is no law.

There is not even responsibility. There is only need, the all-encompassing need to survive. The human animal in his natural state is solely driven by the need to survive. Law is an invention of man arising out of his need to manage society. 'Law' has no other basis of existence other than the society of mans need. Thus we are free to choose the nature and form of the 'Law' we will need to serve us.

Fact. In the natural order there is no morality.

There is only the need to procreate. The male of the species is driven by the need to acquire the female of the species and procreate. Morality is an artificial construction entirely created by man and without purpose other than social order. The long experience of mans journey through history has however demonstrated that the morality which derives from the Christian Bible is more likely to produce an adequate society than any other differently derived system.

Man is simply an animal with special gifts and in any consideration of what should be the criteria that govern the responsibilities of man, then that unalterable truth must be born in mind. Because man is an animal and therefore subject to the same rules of genetic selection as are all other animals, then of necessity the teeming millions of men will be divided by wide chasms of ability and understanding.

<u>Fact. In the natural state there are no such thing as human rights.</u>

Any human animal born into this world will only survive that first day of life with the express permission of those other human animals that surround it. The concept that somewhere there are basic human rights encodified in a table and carved in tablets of stone is a destructive and entirely false belief. We are free to construct a table of human rights that satisfy our perception of justice and they will exist only on that basis.

Man is unique among all animals in possessing intellectual consciousness and the ability to communicate in a comprehensive manner; these attributes have enabled man to manipulate his environment to some extent. These attributes have also led man to a position of dominance in the natural order of nature. Using these attributes with only a dimly understood intellectual purpose has created swollen populations whose millions exist in meaningless conflict and developing crisis.

Given his dominance in nature and notwithstanding the limitations of his intellectual understanding of life's purpose, man has invented 'The Law' and invented 'Morality.' This invention takes many forms depending on racial development and variables such as climate and general environment. None of these inventions has a better claim than any other to being 'The Best.'

Having created the swollen populations that in themselves now threaten all mankind's' future, it became necessary for the manipulators of those swollen populations to create 'Law' and 'Morality' in order to manage their perceived interests. The structure of the various society's established, is an arbitrary one generated without forward purpose, but driven by cliché need, none of which has a particular claim for excellence or performance standards that are in any way justifiable except by imposed authority.

Because the history and mythos of 'Human Rights' 'The Law' and 'Morality' are now inextricably mixed with pseudo religious and cult abnormalities, mankind is no longer valuing these human inventions as generated tools but has come to regard them as divine realities. This unrealistic view of what are essentially; simply mechanisms of management has, and is, distorting society in a direction that will end in disaster. Man the animal has a wide range of intellectual understanding, ranging from near idiocy to super intelligence, and as a consequence of his flawed understanding of 'purpose' refuses to separate these wide variations and insists that all are equal. This direction of human management is laced with the seeds of catastrophe.

In the full treatise of this manuscript the provisions described herein are fully justified and more fully explained.

Final Note. Anyone who is not a definition '2' racialist is a dangerous fool and an enemy of civilisation.

This book was written over a number of years, in fact the period from 2003 until the current year 2016.

As a consequence the book contains a number of anachronisms, reference is made to President Obama before election and Nelson Mandela before and after his death.

These references have been left as written because they do not devalue the narrative.

Tomas Jimenez Garcia.

December 2016.

69356712R00095

Made in the USA
Columbia, SC
18 April 2017